COMPETITIVE STRATEGY

LeaderCrest Academy

COMPETITIVE STRATEGY

A CONTEMPORARY RETAKE

C B RAO

LEADERCREST ACADEMY

Notion Press

Old No. 38, New No. 6
McNichols Road, Chetpet
Chennai - 600 031

First Published by Notion Press 2016
Copyright © C B Rao 2016
All Rights Reserved.

ISBN
Hardcase: 978-1-946436-86-3
Paperback: 978-1-946436-68-9

This book has been published with all efforts taken to make the material error-free after the consent of the author. However, the author and the publisher do not assume and hereby disclaim any liability to any party for any loss, damage, or disruption caused by errors or omissions, whether such errors or omissions result from negligence, accident, or any other cause.

No part of this book may be used, reproduced in any manner whatsoever without written permission from the author, except in the case of brief quotations embodied in critical articles and reviews.

Dedicated to

*Professor **L V L N Sarma**, Ph.D.*

*Professor **M Durgaprasada Rao**, MBA*

My management gurus at Indian Institute of Technology Madras

and

*Professor **Michael E Porter**, Ph.D.*

My (indirect) strategy guru at Harvard Business School

Other Books by the Author

1. From Start-up to Ramp-up: Indian Insights and Global Context
2. Technology and Competitive Strategy: Perspectives for Innovators, Differentiators and Followers

Table of Contents

Introduction
Competitive Strategy: An Enduring Thesis..*xi*

Chapter 1
A Theory of Competitive Economic Forces... 1

Chapter 2
Liquidity, the Potent Competitive Force 8

Chapter 3
From Competition to Collaboration 18

Chapter 4
Structural Analysis, Strategic Groups and Mobility Barriers.............. 28

Chapter 5
Buyer Power and Firm Competitiveness 36

Chapter 6
Supplier Power and Firm Competitiveness 44

Chapter 7
A Framework of Competitive Moves 53

Chapter 8
Theory of Market Signalling... 61

Chapter 9
Competitor Clusters and Competitor Analysis 70

Chapter 10
Competitive Strategy and Competitor Analysis 80

Chapter 11
Structural Analysis and Industry Definition 89

Chapter 12
Cost Leadership and Quality Leadership 102

Chapter 13
Differentiation and De-Commoditisation 109

Chapter 14
Niche as a Core Competence 117

Chapter 15
Strategic Comparators and Responders 126

Epilogue
The Strategically Balanced Corporation *137*

Bibliography *145*

About the Author *147*

Introduction

Competitive Strategy: An Enduring Thesis

Competitive Strategy: Adapting to Dynamic Times Enhances Proven Strengths

- Michael Porter's treatise on Competitive Strategy and the Five Forces Model, though formulated in 1980, remains a highly educative guidance on strategy and structure.
- However, the theory does not directly address the effects of a volatile global economic environment, disruptive digital technologies and consequent changes in industrial structure.
- This book focuses on reviewing the key tenets of Competitive Strategy and identifies ways in which the models and constructs can be further reinforced by incorporating economic, technological and business forces in new models.
- It also deals with the several interrelationships that influence firm-level positioning and strategies in the bid for competitive advantage in the marketplace and provides additional approaches for strategy formulation and execution.

Professor Michael Porter contributed significantly to the field of strategy through his path-breaking books, *Competitive Strategy: Techniques for Analyzing Industries and Competitors* (1980), *Competitive Advantage: Creating and Sustaining Superior Performance* (1985), and *The Competitive Advantage of Nations* (1990). The first book deals with strategy in the context of an industry and the second discusses how firms can build competitive advantage by applying competitive strategy techniques. The third book contributes at a macro level, analysing and hypothesising how nations can build competitive advantage. There have been important contributions to the field of strategy from other scholars, for example, Prahalad (1990, 1994), Hamel (1989) and Hammer (1993). Some of these and other works are listed in the Bibliography. However, there is, perhaps, no set of works as expansive and integrated as Porter's in approaching the myriad complexities of strategy. Porter's treatises on competitive strategy and competitive advantage provide a powerful array of concepts and analytical techniques that can help craft meaningful business strategies.

Among the three books, the first treatise on Competitive Strategy remains the more profound and fundamental theory and practice of strategy. This book of mine, *Competitive Strategy: A Contemporary Retake*, reviews Porter's overall work and evaluates the enduring relevance of his thesis. It examines in detail some major facets of Porter's work in terms of their appropriateness to current and futuristic business environments. Although Porter has since updated his book, the style and substance remain unchanged from the work of 1980. It is for this reason that this review anchors around the foundational work of 1980. Porter's work on Competitive Strategy, with its focus on competition and competitiveness at firm and industry levels, makes two fundamental contributions, along with many other supportive ones. The first is a theory of competitive forces, which is one of the most elegant ever expounded in the field of management. It uniquely hypothesises the relationships between the firm and the environment and between firms in an industry. Porter identified five forces of competition, namely, the threat of new entrants, threat of substitute products or services, bargaining power of buyers, bargaining power of suppliers and intensity of industry rivalry. Porter's Five Forces Theory draws largely on the structure-conduct-performance theories of industrial economics. Porter held that the five competitive forces vary based on the nature of the industry, the state of the industry and the state of the firm (See Figure I.1).

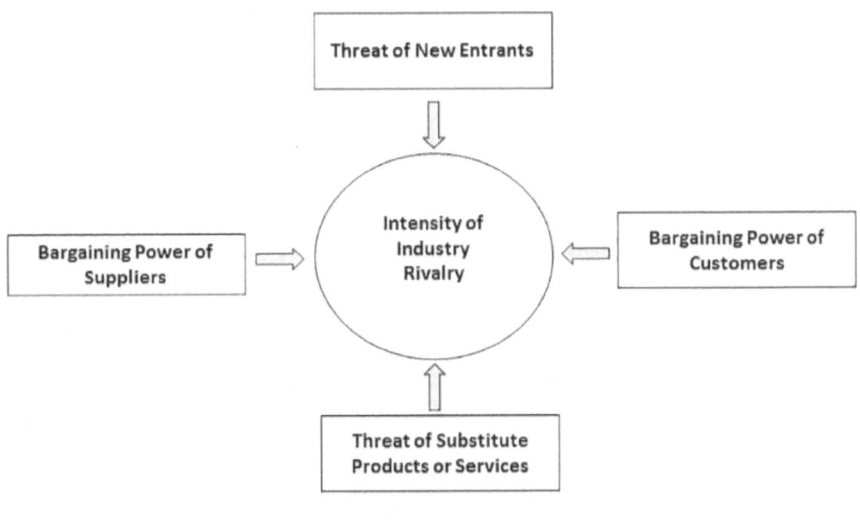

Figure I.1
Porter's Five Forces Model

The second fundamental contribution of Porter's work has been in terms of competitive strategies that are appropriate for most industries and their several phases of evolution. Porter proposed them as cost leadership, differentiation and niche (or focus). These are conceptually and practically elegant. Any firm that has cost leadership can ensure price competitiveness or earnings superiority or a combination thereof with certain *inter se* trade-offs. A firm that follows differentiation can achieve a superior market and price position based on a set of differentiated features. A firm that follows a niche strategy seeks to adopt narrow product-market strategies that are unique to it. Some firms are successful in adopting a mix of the three strategies for different product-market segments to eventually emerge as industry leaders.

Michael Porter also held that definition of the industry in which a firm operates and the levels of entry and mobility barriers within and across defined industries also influence competitive strategy. Strategies of integration and diversification within an industry are proposed to influence and be influenced by the five forces. In a manner of speaking, Porter's theory of competitive strategy represents a domain at the intersection of industrial structure and business performance. In his expansive work, he lists a number of factors that influence strategy and structure. Another important contribution is in terms of developing models of competitive strategy relevant to different phases of industry evolution. While the areas of discussion are many, the model of five competitive forces and the three generic strategies in a framework of structural analysis constitute the core.

This book on Competitive Strategy is based on my belief that while Porter's strategy framework is enduring, global economic forces that have been affecting businesses and their strategies from the mid–2000s need to be recognised. Conventional structures of industry have been undergoing a significant change due to developments in information, telecommunication and broader digital technologies, a trend that must also be factored in. I believe that Porter's excellent conceptual and analytical framework needs to be adapted to respond to the dramatic shifts in economic and technological environments. This book focuses primarily on recapping and reviewing select portions of Porter's work on Competitive Strategy in the context of economic forces and developing supplemental constructs to strengthen the core analytical framework.

The book embeds the impact of technology on competitive strategy throughout but recognises that a more focused and detailed analysis of the same has been presented in my companion work, *Technology and Competitive Strategy: Perspectives for Innovators, Differentiators and Followers* (2016). That work analyses how technology directly affects competitive strategy through five forces of technology and how firms could respond with technology-driven competitive strategies. It also develops customised constructs of technology-strategy-structure relationships. As such, this book focuses elaborately on the impact of economic and industrial forces on competitive strategy, absorbing technology-specific insights wherever appropriate.

Other factors such as people, management and investment also operate as primary or secondary drivers of competitive forces. Much has been written about these factors. Given that technology and economy, which have begun to exert a much greater impact on strategy from the mid–2000s, have not received due attention in the theory of competitive strategy, I strongly believe in the need for focused additional constructs. Together with the earlier book on technology, this book addresses these two transformational shifts.

The book, which is organised as fifteen chapters and an epilogue, examines and evaluates the multiple ways in which the changes in environment over the past four decades redefine competitive forces and redraw competitive strategy with a specific emphasis on the macro environment.

Chapter 1, A Theory of Competitive Economic Forces, discusses how a volatile economic environment affects a firm's strategic positioning and structural ability. It identifies five important economic forces—the threat of inflation, the risk of global capital flows, the bargaining power of national technologies, the bargaining power of national markets and the intensity of national rivalry—and suggests a 'micro model within macro model' approach.

Chapter 2, Liquidity, the Potent Competitive Force, identifies global liquidity as the most potent of the five economic forces. As an alternative to the 'model within model' approach of Chapter 1, it proposes incorporation of global liquidity as the sixth competitive force to supplement the five forces model. The chapter argues that as firms become huge national assets, the need for such firms to recognise system liquidity as an essential competitive force becomes even more intense.

Chapter 3, From Competition to Collaboration, discusses how networking is affecting the transformation of traditional industrial structures and proposes a model of five collaborative forces, comprising competition-driven market expansion, the collaborative power of substitute products or services, the collaborative power of customers (buyers), the collaborative power of suppliers and the balance of collaborative synergy and competitive rivalry.

Chapter 4, Structural Analysis, Strategic Groups and Mobility Barriers, reviews how Porter proposes drawing of strategic groups based on strategic dimensions and proposes relative dimensioning as a more insightful option. Strategic grouping becomes an excellent predictor when the industry is defined through a few dominant dimensions that are the most important in terms of strategic calibration.

Chapter 5, Buyer Power and Firm Competitiveness, proposes that instead of attempting to reduce buyer power, firms should engage with buyers continuously to serve them better. It demonstrates multiple ways in which leaders and employees can support positive engagement and proactive collaboration with customers or buyers and derive several benefits to firms. It highlights the importance of product design and delivery in the new framework.

Chapter 6, Supplier Power and Firm Competitiveness, takes a new perspective on supplier power by proposing that despite their difference in ownership and value chains, suppliers and firms are integrated by technology. It addresses key challenges in the firm-supplier relationship, one of which is the development of a fine balance between proprietary technology (as a market-dominating factor) and freedom to operate (as a risk-mitigating factor).

Chapter 7, A Framework of Competitive Moves, proposes an analytical framework that crystallises a new theme: players in the industry must first be classified on the basis of their positioning in terms of their core competencies and the contingent business results. It advocates understanding the firm and competitors in terms of two constructs. The first is a two-dimensional competitor typology and the other, a nine-grid market-moving matrix.

Chapter 8, Theory of Market Signalling, discusses how the theory of market signalling is vitiated by the volatility in global economic conditions. It cautions firms not to search for signals when strategies are obvious in the contemporary business environment. It also highlights that seemingly innocuous signals could be harbingers of resolutely incredible strategies.

Chapter 9, Competitor Clusters and Competitor Analysis, outlines the differences between the outside-in and inside-out approaches to studying competitors. The chapter discusses the importance of strategic groups and competitor clusters in understanding competitor excellence or the lack of it. It hypothesises that strategic group is a good target to benchmark entry but competitor cluster is a relevant concept to gauge competitive response.

Chapter 10, Competitive Strategy and Competitor Analysis, reviews Porter's three generic strategies of cost leadership, differentiation and focus. It hypothesises that generic competitive strategies can transform into firm-specific competitive advantage only by integrating technology and talent in strategy formulation rather than through scale and scope. A unique analytical framework of cost leadership-differentiation is proposed.

Chapter 11, Structural Analysis and Industry Definition, discusses the challenges faced in industry definition in the context of digital disruption of industries and breakdown of traditional barriers. It identifies the four ways in which industries are affected (reinforcement, reconfiguration, transformation and re-invention) and the need for the theory of competitive forces to be linked to how industries are disrupted.

Chapter 12, Cost Leadership and Quality Leadership, analyses the true import of cost leadership and cautions firms against viewing cost leadership independent of quality leadership. It discusses how firms move into cost-quality clusters and how technology and management act as the integrators of cost and quality. Rendering the highest quality work at the lowest possible cost, and in the shortest possible timeframe, differentiates a firm from others in the industry.

Chapter 13, Differentiation and De-commoditisation, discusses differentiation alongside its antithesis, commoditisation, made more commonplace by the availability of platform technologies in the marketplace. While not all firms may have the resources to become differentiators, many firms can develop ways to fight commoditisation, the chapter argues. Three ways of de-commoditising (by value, function or retro-design) are proposed in the chapter.

Chapter 14, Niche as a Core Competence, compares niche as a strategy in the past with current approaches. It outlines that a niche strategy cannot be static and needs to be constantly improvised. In many instances, certain unique capabilities of firms help develop niche strategy. The chapter concludes that niche is nothing but the core competency of a firm translated into focused product, marketing or other functional strategies.

Chapter 15, Strategic Comparators and Responders, argues that traditional strategic planning processes are rigid and introverted even with competitive benchmarking and internal metrics. The chapter proposes a construct of strategic comparators (metrics and scenarios) and responders (reactive strategies), which are like dots in the environment, and suggests that strategy formulators should have the ability to connect the dots faster and better.

The **Epilogue, The Strategically Balanced Corporation,** observes that most strategic prescriptions including competitive strategy are focused on relentless growth. It proposes the concept of a Strategically Balanced Corporation that seeks balance within each function and among functions. It proposes that such a corporation is able to move through economic and business cycles successfully while exploiting opportunities with agility.

I believe that the discussions, examples and hypotheses as well as the models, constructs and formats detailed in this book illuminate the fascinating and exciting ways in which the volatile and rapidly changing economic and business environment can shape competitive strategy. With adequate contextual focus laid on technology as a direct driver of competitive strategy, the book presents a more comprehensive appreciation together with my earlier companion book on Technology and Competitive Strategy.

I sincerely hope that this book will inspire professionals and business leaders as well as academicians and public policy makers involved in strategy and growth to appreciate issues and solutions in a broader industrial and economic context.

C Bhaktavatsala Rao

Chennai

December 01, 2016

Chapter 1
A Theory of Competitive Economic Forces

When Global Economic and National Forces Become Overwhelming: The Theory of Competitive Strategy Needs an Overarching Model

- Porter's theory of five competitive forces is powerful and elegant; however, it needs reinforcement to reflect current and emerging realities.
- The new reality is that competitive forces or their sources cannot be viewed in discrete silos; there are many overlaps and interfaces.
- Firm-level competitive strategy is today overwhelmed by a paradigm of economic forces, national aspirations and technological changes that affect industrial structure and performance.
- Firms must be cognisant of the big differences between national economic forces and industrial competitive forces and the top-down impact of economic forces on business strategy.

Michael Porter's Theory of Competitive Strategy (1980) is undoubtedly a landmark thesis in the domain of strategy, uniquely expressing the relationships between a firm and the environment as well as between firms in an industry. Professor Porter identified five forces of competition—threat of new entrants, threat of substitute products or services, bargaining power of buyers, bargaining power of suppliers and intensity of industry rivalry—that could have a huge impact on the competitive strategy of a firm. Porter's Five Forces Theory draws largely on the structure-conduct-performance theories of industrial economics. Porter held that the five competitive forces vary based on the nature of the industry, the state of the industry and the state of the firm. He advocated that firms could deploy three generic strategies—cost leadership, differentiation and niche—to derive sustainable competitive advantage over competitors.

Michael Porter also held that the definition of the industry in which a firm operates in and the levels of entry and mobility barriers within and across defined industries influence a firm's competitive strategy. He proposed that strategies of integration and diversification within an industry influence, and are influenced by, the five forces. In a manner of speaking, Porter's theory of competitive strategy represents a domain at the intersection of industrial structure and business performance. Path-breaking though Porter's theory has been, there are certain critical shortcomings, especially with reference to contemporary industrial development. The first shortcoming is in viewing buyers, suppliers and competitors as distinct, unrelated entities. The second is the proposition that the higher the entry barrier, the greater the value or profit potential. The third is the idea that industry or environmental volatility is low and predictable, enabling firms to plan their competitive strategies based on structural designs. Fourthly, and more importantly, it is not calibrated to address contemporary economic realities.

New realities

The new realities are that buyers, suppliers and competitors have multiple overlaps. In an industry, firms competing at the product level tend to collaborate at component or material level. While they may look for sourcing advantages or cost savings, brand premiums or sales discounts and design dependencies or independencies, they also tend to be aligned to maximise the overall throughput individually and collectively. The smart device industry is an example, with multiple layers of collaboration at the component level amidst competition at the product level. Secondly, entry barriers need not necessarily represent value-building opportunity. The steel industry might have the highest investment intensity and hence, the highest entry barriers but typically offers meagre returns compared to low investment industries such as fast-moving consumer goods (FMCG). Thirdly, industry structures are increasingly affected by economic trends, even as economic trends themselves are increasingly governed by commodity and liquidity cycles as well as cross-border investments and exchange rate regimes, which are all becoming increasingly volatile, affecting the stability of strategies.

The new realities could also combine two or more competitive forces into one and accentuate their combined impact. For example, new firms could enter the industry with substitute products or services (not just imitator products), thus increasing the competitive intensity more than proportionately. Buyers may start dumping their products in product exchange or refurbished product schemes, thus making firms substitutional rather than incremental sellers. Industry rivalry could be more intense due to exit barriers (absence of bankruptcy provisions) rather than low entry barriers. Commodity and other economic cycles may vary the impact on strategies, such as cost leadership, at the design or manufacturing level, from time to time. An automotive design strategy developed at great cost for maximal fuel economy may become less powerful in a protracted phase of extremely cheap oil prices. Low global metal and mineral prices can completely alter the economics of firms in related product spaces. China's exit from basic chemicals may present exceptional opportunities that Indian firms may have failed to anticipate adequately.

Macro versus micro

For Porter, an industry-specific and firm-mediated microenvironment provided for sharper articulation of corporate and business strategies, compared to woolly Strength-Weaknesses-Opportunities-Threats (SWOT) analyses that were in fashion in the 1960s and 1970s. The issue is whether an industry-level micro-environment as proposed by Porter in the 1980s is still appropriate for formulating competitive strategy in the context of strong and volatile trends buffeting the macro-environment over the past decade. The way the global economy anticipates US Fed rate hikes or the entire Indian industry is anchored around an RBI rate cut indicates that macroeconomic factors have an increasingly overarching influence these days. Similarly, the way the slowdown in China causes global demand tremors and stock market blues or a taxation issue frays or calms the nerves of portfolio investors in India are also proof of global economic and industrial interconnectivity.

Industries and firms are affected not merely by relevant competitive forces but also by national and international economic forces. In India, Initial Public Offerings (IPOs) as well as follow-on offerings and stake sales by Public Sector Undertakings (PSUs), for example, are affected by volatility in stock market sentiments, which are, in turn, caused by global economic and liquidity headwinds. Economic liberalisation, implemented progressively from 1992, may have freed industrial development from public policy (notwithstanding residual macro regulations) but contemporary industrial development is affected more than ever by national and international economic factors. There is probably no way to decouple the Indian economy and industry from such vagaries but there must at least be a model that focuses the attention of firms and industries on such competitive economic forces. This chapter proposes a theory of five competitive economic forces as an adjunct to Porter's theory of competitive strategy.

Five economic forces

Five important economic forces affect industrial structure and performance: the threat of inflation, the risk of global capital flows, the bargaining power of national technologies, the bargaining power of national markets and the intensity of national rivalry. Each of these has an impact on industry-level competitive strategy. They also dictate a preferred drift in the generic competitive strategies. Figure 1.1 illustrates the model.

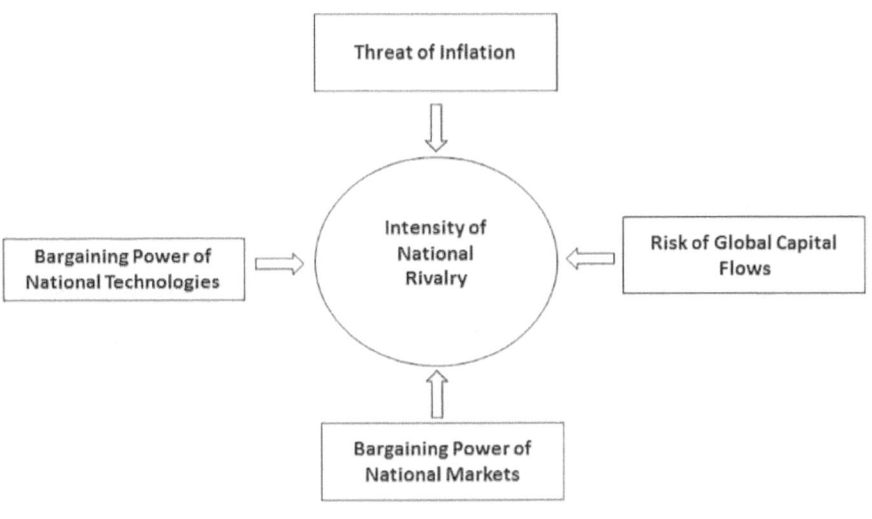

Figure 1.1
Five Economic Forces Model

The competitive threat of inflation, for example, affects the bargaining power of suppliers as well as buyers. It also supports cost leadership as a preferred generic competitive strategy. The competitive force of global capital flows influences market capitalisation levels on bourses, and brings in (or drives out) risk capital for expansion and diversification. Unlimited capital flows take the focus away from cost leadership and promote differentiation and niche as generic competitive strategies.

Nations play a major role in licensing or attracting technologies and generate major bargaining power over these. This is countered in part by the bargaining power of national markets. This interplay is evident usually in military technologies, for example, the Rafale aircraft deal between France and India or the more recent opening up of Foreign Direct Investment (FDI) in defence and other sectors subject to Make in India covenants. Globally too, national efforts extended to high-end civilian technologies as well (for example, China's high-speed rail technology for US to connect Los Angeles and Las Vegas). The enthusiasm at industry level to partake in Indian markets was evident when major US technology firms vied with each other during Prime Minister Narendra Modi's visit to the US West Coast in

September 2015. When nations compete to participate in emerging markets, rivalry is heightened but to the benefit of local industry. Governments can leverage such rivalry for national benefit. India, for example, can benefit from generating international interest and rivalry for building bullet-train infrastructure or creating new capital cities.

Before applying Porter's Five Forces Theory for competitive strategy, a firm must, therefore, apply the Five Economic Forces Theory to establish the correct perspectives for firm-level competitive strategic analysis.

Model within model

The above discussion proposes, probably for the first time in strategic management, a theory of competitive economic forces as an overarching umbrella under which Porter's theory of competitive strategy must be recalibrated. The major difference between national economic forces and industrial competitive forces is that the former are more volatile and unpredictable and also susceptible to public policy and government actions as well as geo-political vicissitudes. While industrial competitive forces are more predictable, they are swayed by changes in the economic policy framework. As a contemporary example, the economic and industrial impact arising from the decision of Narendra Modi Government in India on November 8, 2016 to withdraw the high-value currency notes of Rs 500 and Rs 1000 from legal tender in an effort to stamp out black money and fake money is an illustration of how economic policies can impact firm level competitive strategies. Further research is needed to understand how the economic forces model can be linked to the industrial forces model. One option could be to choose a time horizon that starts with a major economic inflexion point, model the industrial forces until the expected next inflection point and develop a calibrated industry- and firm-level model for the target timeframe. This book seeks to present several paradigms to academia, practitioners of management, economists and strategists to establish the importance of and evaluate methodologies for coupling both these models—the new economic and the established industrial!

For India, at this point, a combination of competitive economic forces sets up the five force economic model. These forces are variations in inflation (related to strong RBI rate policies as has been evident for some time now), fluctuations in global portfolio investments (driven by global liquidity and quantitative easing), dependence on foreign technologies (for next-generation infrastructure), consumerisation of markets (with increased purchasing power) and increasing national rivalry to enter or expand in India (virtually every developed country wants a share of India). Such an analytical framework sets the tone for recalibrating the basic Porter model. In the ultimate analysis, the issue is not one of choosing between a micro or macro model. The macro model is the missing piece in the current strategy framework and must be expressly provided for, as suggested herein. In addition, Porter's micro model remains relevant but with two caveats. Firstly, industrial play is not only about forces of competition; it should equally be about forces of collaboration. Secondly, the five competitive forces and the entities causing them are not independent of each other but could have overlaps and could be accentuated or attenuated based on overlaps.

Chapter 2
Liquidity, the Potent Competitive Force

Global Liquidity: Solid Support or Volatile Vortex?

- The global economic meltdown of 2008 and the continuing volatility offer significant lessons for companies and for strategy formulation in particular.
- Global economic liquidity is the most powerful of the five economic competitive forces.
- If a two-layer modelling is found to be complex, global liquidity should be added as the sixth force to the classic model of five competitive forces.
- The elasticity of system liquidity to economic downturn or upturn would be a critical parameter affecting firm-level competitive strategy.

The previous chapter posits that the model of five competitive industrial or business forces must be interpreted in terms of an overarching model of five economic forces. The five industrial forces are the threat of new entrants, threat of substitute products or services, bargaining power of buyers, bargaining power of suppliers and intensity of industry rivalry. The five economic forces are the threat of inflation, the risk of global capital flows, the bargaining power of national technologies, the bargaining power of national markets and the intensity of national rivalry. The previous chapter also hypothesised how each economic force has a significant impact on how industry- and business-level competitive forces can be influenced. Interestingly, the common thread among the five economic forces is that they are influenced by, and are susceptible to, government policies. The decision by the Government of India on withdrawal of high value currency notes is a prime example. The decision to move towards a less-cash society, and eventually a cashless society, should open up major opportunities for a number of companies including but not limited to digital payment, fintech, banking and re-skilling businesses while challenging the industries and businesses that are based on cash transactions.

Government policies are constantly seeking global superiority even as the relative economic performance of nations ensures that global economies are in a state of perpetual disequilibrium. Governments and central banks are convinced that global liquidity must be maintained to ensure that the despondent forces of disequilibrium are overcome by the euphoric forces of growth. Whether it is Greece at one extreme or the UK at the other, austerity as an economic policy has caused social hardships and consequently, come under public criticism. Similarly, whether it is the USA at one end or Japan at the other, quantitative easing is at the core of economic revival. If one were choosing an economic force that can be labelled the most important, global liquidity would certainly be a frontrunner. For those strategists in enterprises who would probably be more comfortable with a single model, global liquidity can be added as the sixth competitive force to the conventional five forces model.

Fighting Darwinism

The implicit essence of Porter's theory is that corporate competitiveness play is a 'win by some – lose by some' play, where competitively robust and agile firms alone will sustain themselves and grow. In a sense, Porter's theory reflects modern corporate Darwinism where only the fittest would survive. While inequalities persist, there is now a greater awareness than ever before that every person or entity in the global system deserves a place under the sun. Global liquidity, which flows from developed markets to emerging markets based on opportunities, is a great instrument to elevate needy markets. While Porter's theory is an excellent guidepost, it would be fortified by the incorporation of economic liquidity as the sixth competitive force. Without distracting from the economic rigour that Porter brought to corporate strategy, one may say that true economic growth has to be based on foundations that are more broadly based and sustainable than an approach that suggests, if not endorses, the 'survival of the fittest' doctrine.

Sustainable economic growth must envisage equitable growth of all sections of the society and the profitable coexistence of different types of firms, from global conglomerates to local micro-enterprises and from business leaders to front-line workers. The global financial meltdown and economic recession of 2008 and the ongoing debates in the EU on budgetary austerity versus monetary expansion have focussed on the fact that in the globally connected world, macroeconomic stimulus measures are an essential component of global stability. Business inefficiencies and corporate mismanagement have, from time to time, led to an unprecedented evaporation of economic wealth. Deep economic recession and failures of global corporations forced governments to inject trillions of dollars to arrest economic collapse and ease liquidity crises. The economic meltdown has shaken advanced and emerging countries to the roots. It has demonstrated, shockingly, that industries and societies can be swept away if economic liquidity is ignored by incumbent firms in crafting corporate strategies and by regulators in assuring governance standards.

Economic (or system) liquidity

Firms exist through their products and services to stimulate and cultivate customer needs as well as fulfil and service them in an ever-increasing fashion. Customers embrace additional and new products on a continuous basis to elevate their quality of life. Governments committed to economic growth have a stake in the propagation of this corporate-customer virtuous cycle. Firms and customers, however, require financial resources to carry out their respective obligations of manufacture and consumption. The level and sustainability of economic liquidity in the value chain of a firm constitute an essential competitive force. The five competitive forces for a firm as outlined by Porter differentially affect and are affected by the competitive force of system liquidity. When finance becomes scarce, the intensity of rivalry for resources further pushes down the availability of finance and pushes up the cost of finance.

In an environment of economic stringency, customers move away from high-cost premium products to low-cost functional products while firms are faced with increased receivables. Monopoly suppliers dictate their terms of supply while fragmented suppliers suffer extended working capital cycles and uncertain payments. New product development suffers while new entrants delay entry plans. Greater industry volatility and lower industry profitability characterise the industrial system. The financial sector—comprising banking, non-banking finance, home finance, microfinance, insurance, refinance, private equity, venture capital, mutual fund, pension fund, hedge fund and stockbroking firms—faces a quick and inexplicable evaporation of capital in an environment of downturn. The velocity of circulation of capital comes to a screeching halt. Leveraging and derivative instruments with speculative elements collapse as the system adjusts to align a virtual world of escalating financial value with the physical world of excess assets. Capital-output ratios suddenly turn awry and adverse.

Experiencing system liquidity

Needless to say, stringency or buoyancy unrelated to economic fundamentals causes irrational socio-economic behaviour. For customers, liquidity exists essentially through the cash they have and the credit they can generate. The great American housing bubble of 2007–2009 has demonstrated how a credit-driven market exponentially and speculatively expands until an economic downturn leads to institutional collapse and with it, total market collapse. The global consumer is today more appreciative of the need to lead a life that is meaningfully de-leveraged and sufficiently savings driven while the global governments are more open to appreciating the risks of monetary expansion, even if it is pro-stimulus. This implies that in future, the bargaining power of customers would be strong, in either case.

For a firm that is a part of or contributes to the five components of the five forces theory, liquidity exists in terms of not only equity and debt financing but also in terms of the various assets it holds, from research and manufacturing assets to intellectual and goodwill assets. The manner and value of the acquisition and nurturing of these assets and the speed and effectiveness of their commercialisation or monetisation determine the system liquidity that a firm faces. Unfortunately, true economic value is rarely placed on or leveraged from such non-cash assets until a major event like a merger or acquisition (for example, Nokia) or bankruptcy (for example, Kodak) occurs.

In a growth economy, liquidity tends to be a factor of least concern. Entrepreneurs riding on aspirations and financiers splurging capital on ideas provide an intoxicating feel to the economy. Firms and conglomerates spend to grow. The growth thesis in such circumstances, unfortunately, is based on external funding (whether equity or debt) rather than the firm's own cash generation. Stock markets experience irrational exuberance on the back of liquidity flows, with stretched valuations and risky bets. The principle of productivity is erroneously applied, with firms seeking to do far more than what they can achieve through their internal cash generation. Models of corporate strategy such as Porter's Five Forces Model, therefore, need to be expanded to factor in system liquidity as an overarching sixth competitive force. See Figure 2.1 for a pictorial representation of the expanded model.

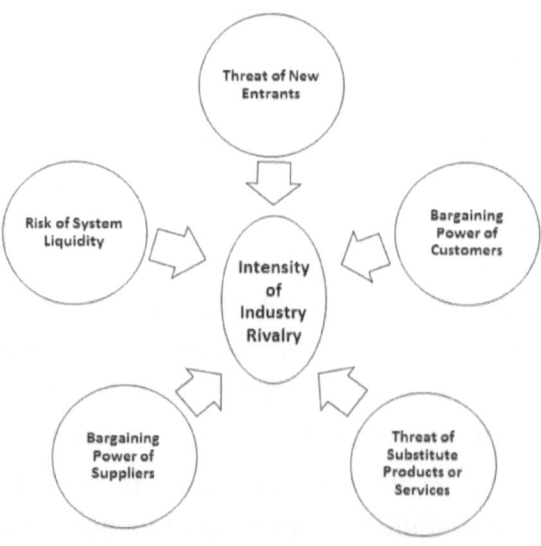

Figure 2.1
Six Forces Model

The Six Forces Model

The fundamental limitation, if one may say so, of Porter's Five Forces Model is that it considers all the participants in the industry, that is, firms, customers, suppliers and new entrants as competitors with conflict of interest in collaborating with each other (relative to the goal of individual profit maximisation). It also considers the creativity of new products as a disruptive force. This model and the underlying assumption may be valid purely from a firm's short-term competitive purpose but is inadequate from a long-term industrial or economic purpose because these forces serve to improve efficiencies and expand markets under certain circumstances.

Porter cites the continued success, by the 1980s, of Paccar in the heavy-duty trucking industry as an illustration of how a firm can achieve sustained long-term profitability by analysing the industry as per the Five Forces strategy and building a competitive position. The example of one firm in an industry, in fact, reinforces the limitation of the Five Forces model. Firms and governments need strategy models that achieve maximal diffusion of economic prosperity. The story in India is different: as long as firms are technically sound they can weather economic cycles despite divergent business models (Ashok Leyland and Tata Motors, for example).

The Six Forces Model factors in system liquidity as the critical core and includes the standard five competitive forces of Porter's model, that is, rivalry, customers, suppliers, entrants and new products as forces that are networked to each other and to system liquidity. The model considers system liquidity as the aggregate financial capability of all four players in the industry, that is, firms, customers, suppliers and entrants, duly modulated by national and global governmental policies. System liquidity, fed not only by the industry but also by the larger economic and financial system, influences and is influenced by the strategies of the firms, customers and suppliers.

Factoring system liquidity

It would be insufficient and even erroneous to consider the profitability of individual industries from a standalone perspective. As Porter rightly observes, industry structure drives competition and profitability irrespective of whether an industry is emerging or mature, high tech or low tech, regulated or unregulated. Moving beyond this, however, firms in strategy-formulation mode have to consider front-end market dynamics and back-end supply dynamics as collaborative factors. By focusing on system liquidity, the Six Forces Model brings in an essential value-chain perspective and a desirable economic perspective to firm-level strategy formulation. Several examples can be provided to support the thesis as below.

Reverting to the US Paccar example of the heavy-duty truck industry, the concept of system liquidity, if applied by all the firms in the industry, integrates the profitability of the total value chain, including the material and component suppliers and the goods transporters. This would enable different players to come up with different strategies in collaborative combinations. While firms clamour for a unified Goods and Services Tax (GST) on the basis of one whole economic value-chain concept, they are diffident about applying the same principle to their operations. Economic value is a total value chain that covers the extraction, conversion and delivery path from the most basic materials and components to the most advanced final product that incorporates the materials and components.

Indian bus makers have languished for decades with low growth rates in production volumes, despite the near doubling of the Indian population, because they have traditionally followed a firm-level competitive strategy (firm against firm) rather than an economy-level systemic strategy (firm as a part of the total national economic system). If a firm in the bus industry develops a strategic methodology to enhance system liquidity, taking along suppliers and customers (passenger transport corporations), the strategy would be more enduring and profitable in the long run. Conversely, if governments bring together bus makers, banks and transport-financing companies and public and private transport operators under one economic value chain, the economic impact would be highly positive.

The Big Three of the US automobile industry have individually and collectively lagged in global competition several times over the past few decades not because of the lack of application of the Five Forces Model but because of a lack of understanding of the total value chain of a complex industry that includes suppliers, dealers and customers as well as oil economics. In contrast, companies such as Toyota as well as several of its competitors in the Japanese automobile industry have turned out superior global performance by viewing themselves as collaborators with their component makers (through concurrent engineering and just-in-time) and customers (through economic and efficient, yet elegant, designs) in a total economic structure.

Retail and distribution companies in developed markets in diverse sectors, including consumer items, that tweaked sourcing strategies for competitive advantage through low-cost sourcing paid dearly with compromised product quality. Some global food and beverage makers, however, prospered by including the farm sector in their strategic planning processes. Despite advance fleet planning and proactive partnerships for aircraft sourcing, global airline firms and the two aircraft makers and their suppliers face repeated crises due to a lack of concern for system liquidity. On the other hand, power projects that have positive relationships with power equipment makers, power distributors and regulators achieve better financial closures and timely project execution.

As firms become huge national assets, the need for them to recognise system liquidity as an essential competitive force becomes even more intense. The battle between the two Ambani brothers in India (Reliance Industries and Reliance Natural Resources), a few years ago, was not, in essence, a battle over price of gas but an unfortunate concomitant of corporate strategies formulated without an appreciation of economic liquidity encompassing gas-using utilities, industrial customers and regulators. While public purpose has no sides to take on private interests, the intertwined economic factors make firm-level competitive strategies a matter of national economic arbitration.

Sanitising business models

Lack of appreciation of systemic liquidity as the sixth competitive force leads companies to develop aggressive strategies that build scale and scope, erect entry barriers, counter suppliers and distributors (at times through integration) and acquire businesses and products. These strategies, all investment intensive, are conceptualised and executed typically during boom times. They are also often financed by external debt and equity financing. Several Indian companies acquired overseas businesses using these competitive strategies.

Dr Reddy's Laboratories, a leading Indian pharmaceutical major, acquired Betapharm of Germany to achieve leadership in the European generics space. Inadequate appreciation of economic liquidity in the European generics market and a high business valuation of the acquisition, which was feebly supported by internal profitability and generously aided by debt, led to severe operating pressures on Dr Reddy's. Tata Steel's Corus acquisition strategy was unsettled by global steel economics on the one hand and UK-specific economic pressures on the other, despite the apparent homogeneity and synergy of technological, product and customer bases. Global generics leader Actavis had to face the pressures of a debt-funded expansion and acquisition spree.

Corporate strategists undoubtedly consider enhanced investments and operational synergies while drafting business models that enhance competitive stakes based on the Five Forces theory. However, system liquidity of the combined value chain must be considered as a sanitiser for the profitability model. If an expansion or acquisition is debt financed or if the expansion or acquisition takes the company into cost-intensive zones, profitability projections would have to be downgraded significantly. The elasticity of system liquidity to economic downturn or upturn would be a critical parameter.

Regulators have a role in ensuring that models of corporate growth are not hijacked by strategic adventurism. The institutional failures that triggered the global meltdown are proof enough of the perils of a totally unregulated play with external funding, whether of the debt or equity variety. Like banking institutions, listed companies should be expected to operate in line with prudent financial and capital adequacy norms relevant for different industries. In addition, listed companies should be subject to 'stress tests' on an annual basis by independent specialist organisations. In the ultimate analysis, firms need to exist and grow not merely to fulfil leadership aspirations but more significantly, for wider economic growth.

The Six Forces Model integrates the competitive force of system liquidity with Porter's classic five competitive forces. It would elevate firm-level corporate strategy into a highly beneficial macro-economic endeavour. Indian firms have to probably encounter new economic liquidity forces not only in the context of currency compression following the demonetization of the high value currency in India but also the rising bond yields and the likely Fed rate increase in the USA. Firms would do well to seek economic optimisation through a model that focuses as much on collaboration as on competition. The next chapter proposes a framework of collaboration within the framework of competitive strategy.

Chapter 3
From Competition to Collaboration

Sustainable Collaboration as a Driver of Positive Competition: Changing Industrial and Competitive Dynamics

- Firms and industries are more networked than ever, collaborating effectively at component level even while competing intensely at product level.
- Design (product) specialisation coupled with market (customer) specialisation exemplifies the new industrial structure.
- It is appropriate to supplement, if not substitute, the five forces model of competition with a model of five collaborative forces relevant to the times.
- Competition must exist but should be more in the nature of product, process and delivery innovation; collaboration helps firms share resources while retaining a distinct identity.

As Charles Darwin hypothesised, the human race is governed by the 'survival of the fittest' dictum. Corporations, the new icons of the progress of civilisation, reflect this dictum to an even greater degree. It is not surprising, therefore, that Michael Porter's works on Competitive Strategy, which seek to advise corporations on strategies to gain a competitive advantage over other firms, have been runaway hits. Although more than thirty years have passed since they appeared on the strategy scene, Porter's theories continue to dictate management thought in the strategy domain. Quite apart from the need to incorporate economic factors, as discussed in the previous chapters, two major inadequacies need to be addressed. Firstly, generic strategies are now well understood by, and remain applicable to, all corporations. Focused execution rather than strategy formulation *per se* determines relative success among corporations. Secondly, in a resource-constrained economic situation, emphasis on fiery competition, which consumes continuous investments by all players, becomes self-defeating over time.

The Five Forces Theory identifies the following five forces as the determinants of the level of competition in an industry: the threat of new competition, the threat of substitute products or services, the bargaining power of customers (buyers), the bargaining power of suppliers and the intensity of competitive rivalry, all analysed within the framework of an industry. Porter's framework brims with the spirit of competition, wherein each stakeholder is constantly jockeying to get the better of a relationship, strategic or tactical. In a sense, Porter's Five Forces Theory is like Theory-X of organisational behaviour, bringing out the negative nuances of corporate growth and economic development. Industry environment and technological attributes have changed so dramatically over the past ten years that the traditional (including Porter's) view of firms and industries 'not talking to or listening to' each other is no longer valid. The Porter Model clearly needs to be redefined to meet new environmental requirements in terms of collaboration, rather than competition.

Networked industries and firms

Today, industries and firms are more networked than ever. Firms are communicating through social networking sites such as Facebook, Google, LinkedIn, YouTube, WhatsApp and Twitter, which are now developing applications for smart devices and computers made by others. The recent Apple iPhone and Apple Watch launches saw Apple collaborating with leading gaming and fitness companies. These are visible examples of networked firms collaborating to develop business jointly. The scenario of a few operating systems supporting a wide variety and range of cellular phones no longer smacks of monopoly domination; instead, it suggests a move to enhance aggregate business potential by enabling others' businesses through individual core competencies. Nothing illustrates this better than Microsoft releasing its productivity suites to all devices. Today, search engines, navigation systems and electronics manufacturers support a mechanical equipment industry such as automobile like never before. The use of electronics in automobiles has improved user luxury and comfort, in addition to safety and convenience. The cars currently manufactured contain more than 1,000 electronic components. With autonomous driving on the anvil, the trend of automobile digitisation will increase even further.

Along with specialisation and competition came the need for firms to diversify their market base to sustain economics. A specialist in forgings needs an expanded market base, forging parts for giant ships as well as small scooters. Similarly, end-product manufacturers began to concentrate on only certain core competencies for themselves, leveraging others' core competencies to finish products. At the same time, the way product profiles and customer needs are matched has diversified in terms of convergence (many needs fulfilled by one device), specialisation (one device for a predominant need), redundancy (many devices for one need) and diversity (many needs and many products). Figure 3.1 illustrates potential combinations.

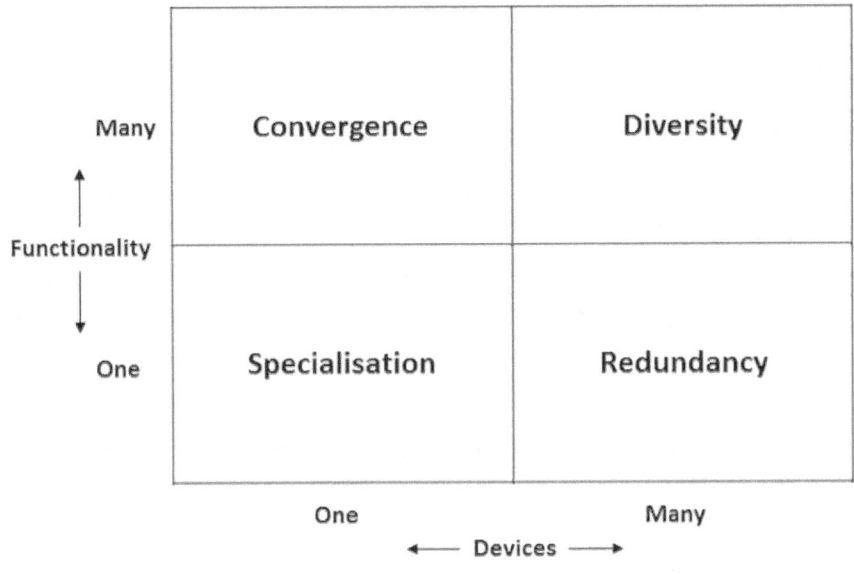

Figure 3.1
Device-Functionality Profiles

Device-functionality trends are prompting firms to develop their own networking strategies to share resources and optimise tactics in the context of continuously changing customer dynamics. Whichever way the current industrial environment is viewed, competition is tempered with collaboration. A strategic theory that redefines the forces governing the industry in terms of collaboration is, therefore, proposed. The collaborative model includes the systemic economic benefits of collaboration as an appropriate dimension in the context of the earlier discussion on the interplay between economic conditions and industrial competitive forces.

Six forces of collaboration

In the new collaborative paradigm, the six forces of collaboration can be stated as: the competition-driven market expansion, the collaborative power of substitute products or services, the collaborative power of customers (buyers), the collaborative power of suppliers, the balance of collaborative synergy and competitive rivalry, and the network of economic synergy, all analysed within the framework of a networked industry definition. This model is appropriately termed the Six Forces Theory of Collaboration. The collaborative model differs from the competitive model in a few important aspects. It sees competition less as an unsettling force and more as a driver of market expansion. It views new products as a bundling opportunity for existing products and as a transition to enhanced customer experience. It also views customers and suppliers as being collaborative, rather than combative, with the firm. Finally, it proposes that collaboration and competition coexist in a firm, with the balance between the two forces determining the growth energy and sustainability of the industry as a whole.

In the collaborative model, industry is not narrowly defined as in Porter's competitive model. For example, the Porter model encourages us to define the automobile industry narrowly in terms of car, truck, bus and motorcycle on the basis that each product is not a substitute for the other. The collaborative model, on the other hand, considers all passenger-serving industries as a holistic one, including not only traditional automobile segments such as car, bus and motorcycle but also supportive industries such as navigation, electronics, telecommunication and entertainment. Similarly, content developers, content makers and content distributors are no longer operating as silos. This may lead to complexity of analysis based on boundless collaboration, moving away from the competitive models of simplicity, based on focused narrowness. However, this is the present reality: complex integration of multiple technologies to provide customer satisfaction, which can be achieved more proficiently and effectively only with collaboration.

Six forces illustrated

The six collaborative forces are grounded in the reality of contemporary and emerging competition as illustrated below (See Figure 3.2).

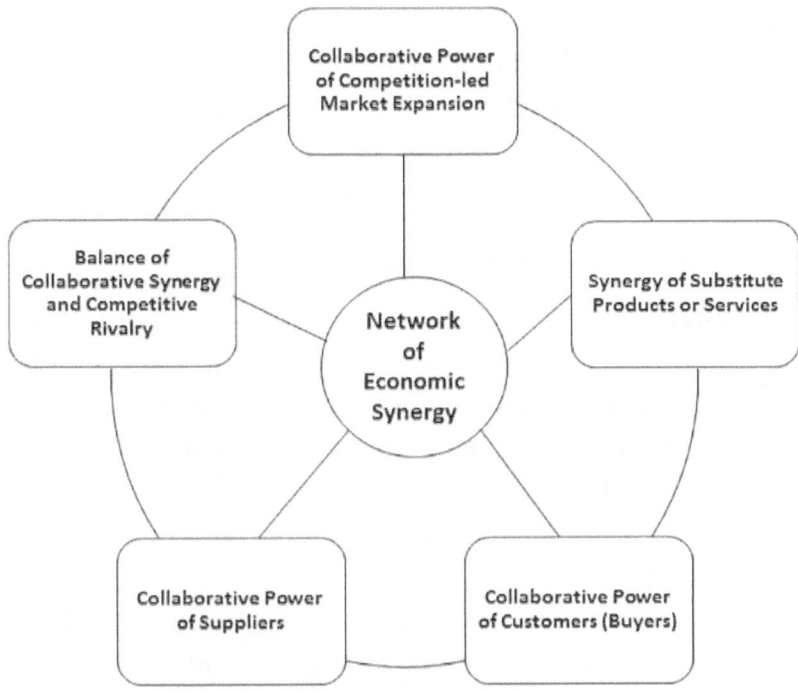

Figure 3.2
Six Collaborative Forces Model

Competition-led market expansion

New competition, in an industry scenario of well-balanced players only serves to expand the market. In India, the entry of new automobile players helped the market grow exponentially, from 500,000 cars per year in the peak Maruti-Suzuki days (late 1990s) to around 3 million cars in 2016. By the same token, the entry of luxury car makers such as Benz, Audi and BMW saw the Indian luxury car market grow to 30,000 from next to nothing, in just five years. Global smartphone sales galloped to 1 billion units in just ten years, again from next to nothing, based essentially on the entry of several smartphone makers in a market amazingly opened up by Apple. The entry of Patanjali with its complete Ayurvedic products will help open a completely new FMCG segment and expand the overall market in India. New competitors offer the unmitigated gift of market expansion to consumers and incumbent players. Even an innovator firm cannot fulfil total market demand in spite of a monopoly position. In an innovative product market segment, such as tablets, for example, the pioneer-leader Apple iPad will have only a one-third share of the 760 million tablets in 2016, according to expert forecasts.

Synergy of substitute products or services

Porter considers substitute products or services to be threats to existing businesses. In fact, except for a few predominantly mechanical apparatuses, such as telex and dot matrix printer, it is unusual for certain basic product concepts to be completely threatened or obliterated. Once the only dominant computing system, the mainframe computer was progressively supplemented by personal computer, laptop, netbook, tablet and ultrabook. Yet, all these computing devices exist in some form or another even today, each gaining from the other's competencies. Convertibles could be the new force in this space. Despite the scorching pace of growth, of around 50 percent per annum, the installed base of tablets could be 1 billion compared to 2 billion personal computers in use, even by 2016. In fact, substitute products help incumbents who are either innovators or smart followers to diversify their product-market segments. Ultrabook is an example of how computers could reinvent themselves by taking design cues from later-generation tablets.

Collaborative power of customers (buyers)

When firms and industries exist for customers, it is ironic that Porter considers them a competitive force. Customer demand, no doubt, leads to competitive entry by other firms or consumers and causes switching between products, brands and firms; in this manner, customers do have a competitive impact. Failure to cater to customer preferences may lead to product atrophy. However, the predominant bond between firms and consumers is, and ought to be, one of collaboration. Consumers simply love a great product and collaborate with the firm by patronising successive generations of products. Firms which view consumers as an extended family through a variety of feedback and feed-forward communication mechanisms have seen consumers provide a major collaborative force for business and technological development. The release of beta versions of new software for consumers is an example of how firms now appreciate the need for consumer involvement to achieve better products for full-scale commercial launch.

Collaborative power of suppliers

The notion that end-product manufacturers are at the mercy of their suppliers is also not relevant in the contemporary scenario. Specialisation in materials and component technologies has enabled component makers to lead new product development. Smartphone makers are increasingly setting up pre-release collaborations with application developers for the right ecosystem. Collaborative planning emphasises an approach by which suppliers and firms work together to avoid over- or under-bidding of positions and instead maximise end-product opportunities in the marketplace with right products, right pricing and right volumes. In fact, bilateral collaboration, between one end-product manufacturer and each component maker, needs to be elevated to a collaborative network that includes everyone in the system.

Balance of collaborative and competitive rivalry

Porter's model assumes that competitive rivalry in an industry increases, as the fifth force, with the number of firms in the industry and the intensity of other competitive forces. However, it is also possible that a few, if not all, of the firms in an industry could collaborate even while competing in the marketplace. Sharing production sites, utilising R&D facilities, sharing marketing channels, warehousing and ground-handling facilities, co-branding and co-marketing, exchanging components and cross-licensing intellectual property, among others, help firms pool resources while keeping individual identities discrete. Such collaboration helps companies bring down costs. An equitable balance between collaboration and competition in an industry occurs as the industry rapidly evolves.

Network of economic synergy

Collaboration does not occur by happenstance. It is a result of the positive behaviour of the five forces that generate an economic synergy in the network. A firm that assiduously avoids markets opened up by new entrants steadfastly refuses to understand the relevance of substitute products. Such a firm concentrates on different groups of buyers for surge buying, toggles between different suppliers for procurement savings, and does not understand the relative merits of collaboration. Competition generates far less economic synergy (in fact, generates negative economic power) relative to a firm that acts positively on all these fronts. A firm should strive to create an ecosystem that adapts to markets expanded by new entrants, utilises new substitute products, develops customer-centric relationships, partners with suppliers for shared growth and respects collaborative competition. As such, collaboration generates a network of economic synergy with a positive collaborative force.

From competition to collaboration

This discussion does not suggest that firms should or can cease competition and that business development is possible only through inter-firm collaboration. Instead, the hypothesis is that all corporate strategy need not be, and should not be, comprised only of a strategy of competition. Competition must exist but more in the nature of product, process and delivery innovation or differentiation. This strategy alone delights customers and expands markets. However, it requires significant investments. The model of collaborative strategy can help firms optimise their investments by sharing resources while retaining a distinct identity. Firms can derive synergy by looking for areas of collaboration with their stakeholders, be they customers or suppliers, and their competitors, whether they are followers in an existing product line or innovators of new substitute products and services. They can also look for collaborations in entirely new fields as well as new methods. For example, in the wake of demonetization in India, collaborative arrangements between the formal sector and the informal sector on the one hand and firms in general and digital payment service providers on the other hand are necessary to utilise the opportunities and overcome the challenges.

While the model of six collaborative forces as enunciated here has significant validity, it is open to further study if it can be followed up with generic collaborative strategies, on the lines of generic competitive strategies. In the collaborative model as well, cost leadership and product differentiation or niche remain the ultimate competitive goals and generic strategies of collaboration are needed to reach these goals. For example, product collaboration, process collaboration and marketing collaboration could be the three principal strategies that competing firms could employ to great advantage. The differentiators for each firm, despite the collaborative sharing, will be design uniqueness, operational excellence and delivery efficiency. That said, uniqueness can be created by two forces joining together to open up an entirely new field in the manner that GSK, the pharmaceutical giant, and Alphabet (the parent company of Google, the Internet giant) collaborated in recent months to establish a new company in the bio-electronics field.

Chapter 4
Structural Analysis, Strategic Groups and Mobility Barriers

Structural Analysis within Industries: Strategic Groups and Mobility Barriers

- Strategic group is an intermediate frame of reference between looking at the firm as a whole and each firm separately; it aids structural analysis.
- Relative dimensioning results in a more perceptive strategic grouping; product specialisation and manufacturing integration are two of the many possible relative dimensions.
- Mobility barriers are intrinsic characteristics of strategic groups and can be interpreted as core competencies for such groups.
- A study of strategic groups provides additional inter-group insights that can be effectively used by firms to improve physical and financial performance.

In his work on Competitive Strategy, Michael Porter postulates that structural analysis at the industry-level provides several useful insights into the five competitive forces and the broad methodologies by which individual firms can manage them. He also suggests that industry-level structural analysis by itself is inadequate to explain why some firms are more profitable than others in the same industry environment. To explain this difference, Porter proposes structural analysis within an industry as a useful adjunct to structural analysis of the industry. He also embeds the concepts of strategy groups and mobility barriers in the study of structural analysis.

Despite the elegance and popularity of Porter's work, no quantitative framework has come up to support Porter's qualitative paradigm of competitive strategy. In 1991, I provided a unique quantitative rigour to Porter's framework. The work focused on the structure and performance of the Indian automobile industry and demonstrated that Porter's theories of competitive forces and competitive strategy would have practical relevance and applicability. While appreciating Porter's creative and utilitarian theories, the work proposed additional observations and constructs relevant to the current and future times. This chapter's focus is on structural analysis, strategic groups and mobility barriers, which are important qualitative concepts expounded by Porter.

Strategic dimensions

Porter's work is highly conceptual and qualitative as well as expansive in its listing. For example, it suggests as many as thirteen strategic dimensions capable of providing companies varied strategic options to differentiate themselves within an industry. These are: specialisation, brand identification, push versus pull, channel selection, product quality, technological leadership, vertical integration, cost position, service, price policy, leverage, relationship with parent company and relationship to home and host governments. Porter states that the level to which each strategic dimension plays out is related to the nature of the industry while in some cases the strategic dimensions are, in fact, related.

Porter also proposes that characterising the strategies of significant competitors in an industry along these dimensions is the first step in structural analysis within industries. This activity, he holds, helps map the industry into strategic groups. Porter defines a strategic group as the group of firms in an industry following the same or similar strategy along strategic dimensions. There can be only one strategic group in an industry, if all firms follow the same strategy or each firm could constitute a strategic group if they follow entirely different strategies. However, this is qualitative rather than quantitative. Also, classifying firms into groups on absolute dimensions such as sales or profits does not provide as much comparative benchmarking as classifying on profitability percentage.

Strategic groups

According to Porter, the strategic group is an analytical device designed to aid in structural analysis. It is an intermediate frame of reference between looking at the firm as a whole and each firm separately. It is claimed that strategic groups can explain more perceptively the differences in performance and profitability of firms. In a concept analogous to entry barriers, Porter proposes mobility barriers that prevent a firm from shifting strategic position from one strategic group to the other. Porter hypothesises that firms in strategic groups with high mobility barriers will have greater profit potential than those in groups with lower barriers. He states that strategic groups and mobility barriers change over time.

Reapplying the concepts of structural analysis, Porter proposes that strategic groups experience all the concepts of industry-level competitive forces, namely, bargaining power of buyers, bargaining power of suppliers, threat of substitutes, threat of entry and rivalry among firms. The firm's profitability is seen as the result of the interplay of common industry characteristics, strategic group characteristics and the firm's position within its strategic group. Other related concepts deal with scale and cost position of strategic groups. Porter proposes structural analysis within industries together with the concepts of strategic groups and mobility barriers as a powerful analytical tool to explain firm profitability.

Relative dimensions

In contrast to Porter's work, this book proposes that relative dimensioning is a superior construct, more perceptive of strategy and hence, and a better qualifier for strategic grouping. Relative dimensions help harmonise the effects of scale and scope. Each of these can be well defined and measured. For example, product specialisation is defined in terms of sales per product family. Manufacturing integration is defined in terms of value added in-house. Import intensity is defined as consumption of imported materials and components as a percentage of sales. Export orientation is defined as export income as a percentage of sales. R&D intensity is seen in terms of R&D expenditure (capital and revenue) as a percentage of sales. Financial leverage is seen in terms of shareholder funds as a percentage of total capital employed. Other leading and lagging indicators could also be considered: for example, patent applications made, patents granted, patents commercialised and new product counts could reflect R&D intensity.

The essence of strategic grouping is to correlate the strategic dimensions of a firm to its performance and scale. It would be interesting to compare a group of firms mapped on the dimensions of product specialisation and manufacturing integration to other groups at different levels in terms of their physical and financial performance. My study of the Indian automobile industry suggests that strategic groups high on product diversification (that is, low on product specialisation) and high on manufacturing integration scored better on physical and financial performance for the period of the study, the 1980s. Similarly, groups low on import intensity and high on export intensity performed better. Groups high on R&D intensity and low on financial leverage also scored well. Creative relative dimensioning helps group the firms in terms of their strategic alignments and related performance parameters.

Overcoming limitations

Since they are two dimensional, strategic groups have limitations in predicting the impact of multiple variables on firm performance. Porter tries to circumvent these limitations by suggesting that strategic groups of firms mapped on any two dimensions could be further elaborated by bubbles that denote the size of the business and the addition of other parameters into the group's description. For example, a strategic grouping drawn on the dimensions of specialisation (narrow line or full line) and vertical integration (high vertical integration or assembly) could be further described in terms of manufacturing cost (low or high), customer service (low or high) and quality (low or high).

Porter's prescription of strategic groups serves more as a descriptive analytical tool rather than a quantitative one.

In contrast, relative dimensions, duly quantified, add depth and breadth to the concept of strategic groups. It doubles the interpretative power of, say, two dimensions to four. It helps strategic grouping become an excellent predictor when the industry can be characterised by a few, preferably two to four, dominant dimensions that are the most important in terms of strategic calibration. For example, in the automobile industry, the relative dimensions of product specialisation and manufacturing integration are two strategic dimensions that could be significantly varied across firms. Other dimensions such as export intensity, R&D intensity and import dependence could help develop additional perspectives. Strategic grouping also works well when there are a number of firms in an industry as this facilitates plotting of the firms into several strategic groups. Figure 4.1 illustrates.

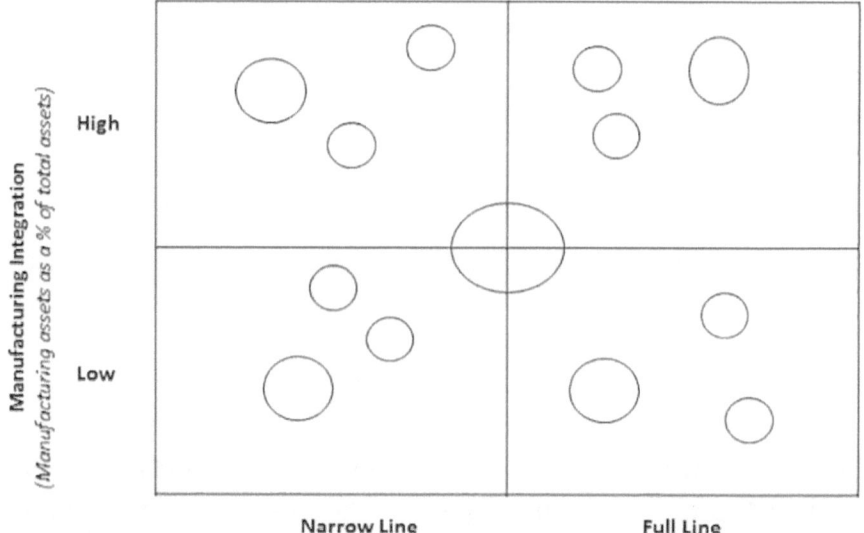

Figure 4.1
Strategic Groups on Relative Dimensions

New foundations

For Porter's strategic grouping to work effectively with quantitative rigour, perceptive strategic dimensioning and customised application to relevant industries is necessary. As with any theory, mere elegance of strategic thinking cannot translate into tangible analytical support unless quantified. The awareness of this limitation enables a better appreciation of the other two concepts: using strategic groups to establish mobility barriers and analyse competitive forces to complete the structural analysis framework.

Physical and financial performance determines the mobility of firms across strategic groups. A firm in a 'high product specialisation and low vertical integration' strategic group should have high financial performance in order to move to a strategic group defined by 'high product diversification and high vertical integration,' which by its very nature requires high capital intensity. If the profitability of such a strategic group is weighed down by other factors, say a heavy dependence on high-cost imports, the firm would face high mobility barriers. Mobility barriers, therefore, are not external to strategic groups but are intrinsic characteristics of strategic groups.

Just as an industry with high entry barriers enables a monopolistic or duopolistic structure with superior profitability, a strategic group with significant entry barriers would have higher potential for profitability. That said, cross-strategic group movement is more common than cross-industry movement. A classic case is in white goods and FMCG industries, where firms constantly seek to move across strategic groups. This is partly because most firms in these industries possess some common attributes in terms of product development and manufacturing capabilities, brand differentiation, investments in trade channels and so on. This enables the typical firm in these industries to bridge mobility barriers. As an axiom, mobility barriers can be interpreted in terms of core competencies required for strategic groups.

Strategic groups and derived power

Firms in strategic groups can get the energy to transcend mobility barriers through derived power. This accrues from being a subsidiary of a major corporation, a part of a major conglomerate or a corporation well-respected by regulatory bodies, including governments. Access to such external power helps firms move into different strategic groups more effortlessly, relative to standalone firms. As an example, Tata Motors would be able to introduce superior quality steel for its automotive use by virtue of having Tata Steel in its conglomerate fold. A subsidiary of a multinational corporation would have the ability to secure better financial leverage or hop across strategic groups requiring higher capital even if its current strategic group has little financial surplus to offer.

Inability to move across strategic groups (or even exit the industry) drives industry consolidation. Equity relationships between needy firms and endowed firms, through mergers and acquisitions, redefine strategic groups. The shifting strategic preferences of firms also lead to structural reconfiguration. The acquisition of Henkel's detergent business by Jyothi Laboratories, LaForge's cement business by Nirma, JP's cement business by Ultratech and JSP's power business by JSW Energy are examples of firms crossing mobility barriers across strategic groups. Mobility across strategic groups has to be carefully thought through to avoid the risk of the acquiring or acquired firm or the merged entity finding itself in a strategic group inferior to the one it belonged to in the pre-consolidation phase.

Globalisation and strategic groups

Globalisation has added an entirely new strategic dimension to this concept. Strategic groups of the same industry tend to vary dramatically across nations. Also, the characteristics of a multinational firm are not automatically exhibited in the same manner in all the countries where the corporation exists (despite the 'One Firm' concept). A corporation that is vertically integrated in the headquarters country need not be so in another country. Understanding of local industrial characteristics helps companies with global corporations become better members of strategic groups. Global developments affect the principal and its subsidiaries differently. Apart from different strategic dimensions pursued across nations, the extent to which countries are coupled (or decoupled) with global economic developments, especially in the developed world, have a major impact on how strategic groups are formed, how they perform and how they reconfigure.

ITC, which started as an Indian subsidiary of a global tobacco giant, has moved into multiple strategic groups including FMCG, hospitality and paper. Hindustan Unilever, the Indian subsidiary of global giant Unilever, is in certain uniquely Indian strategic groups, such as Ayurveda and water purification. Regional firms find it both expedient and necessary to cross the mobility barriers put in place by parent corporations. Regional strategic groups can, in a reverse paradigm, help parent corporations with new internal adjacencies. In a rapidly globalising Indian context, structural analysis, strategic grouping and mobility barriers need to be a dynamic paradigm. Constructing strategic groups on relative dimensions provides additional inter-group insights that firms can use effectively to improve physical and financial performance.

Chapter 5
Buyer Power and Firm Competitiveness

Buyer Power and Firm Competitiveness: Fortune or Poverty in the Marketplace?

- Porter's propositions on buyer power and buyer selection need to be updated in keeping with the times.
- A firm ought to develop its products and services to cater to buyer needs; it should not view buyers as a competitive power.
- Buyers as a group enhance the firm's competitiveness through higher expectations: they neither pressure company resources nor blindly tolerate what companies may offer.
- Wise and effective leaders need to focus really well on only a few things to lead their corporations to glory; product design and product development probably rank highest on that list.

A firm exists because of the buyer. The collective actions of all buyers, to purchase the products and services of all the firms in an industry constitute demand in the marketplace. It is, therefore, counterintuitive to postulate that buyer power is inimical to the interests of individual firms or the overall industry. Michael Porter, however, postulates that buyer power is a competitive force a firm needs to contend with. Together with the other four competitive forces, buyer power determines the level of competitiveness in an industry. Extending the theory further, Porter proposes that most industries sell their products or services not to a single buyer but to a range of different buyers. He holds that the bargaining power of the groups of buyers, viewed in aggregate terms, is a key competitive force determining an industry's potential profitability. Porter believes that the concept of different buyer groups with varying purchasing requirements is valid for producer-goods and consumer-goods industries.

Porter provides a different twist to the concept of market segmentation when he holds that different buyer groups even when they are common to an industry vary widely in terms of purchasing needs, with respect to product quality or durability, customer service, information sought in sales presentations and so on. Buyers are held to differ not only in their structural position but also their growth potential, and hence in the probable growth of their purchase volume. For a variety of reasons, the costs of servicing individual buyers also differ. Porter turns the concept of market segmentation in the context of buyer heterogeneity into a concept of buyer selection by the firm. He argues that a key strategic implication is that a firm can not only find good buyers but also create them. Porter proposes a framework based on four broad criteria to determine the quality of buyers from a strategic standpoint: purchasing need versus company capabilities, growth potential, structural position and cost of servicing. The structural position is expressed in terms of intrinsic bargaining power and propensity to exercise it by demanding low prices.

Contemporary buyer dynamics

As with the other aspects of Porter's theory of competitive strategy, the propositions on buyer power and buyer selection need to be revisited to align with the current times. While designating market opportunity as buyer power may be a creative way of looking at the firm's competitive dynamics, it is also a case of putting the cart before the horse. The idea of a firm selecting its buyers based on its products and services is counterintuitive and rather opportunistic given the fact that the firm ought to develop its products and services to cater to buyers' needs. The proposition that firms try to play on variations or exploit weaknesses in buyers is antagonistic to the contemporary customer-centric view of the firm. In addition, two principles militate against Porter's simplistic but opportunistic buyer power theory. They render Porter's strategy of narrow-line manufacturers searching for buyer segmentation quite suboptimal.

The first principle is that buyers, whether individuals or firms (as buyers themselves), do not have unitary thinking; rather it is individual, social and family thoughts that influence buyers' seemingly individualistic thinking, while it is the collective thinking of professionals in a firm that influence a firm's thought process as a buyer. In developed markets, the purchasing characteristics of industrial buyers are collectively mandated by elaborate firm-level processes and requirements while the purchasing characteristics of retail buyers are highly esteem driven. In emerging markets, notably Asian economies, buyers in firms have great latitude to decide on their purchasing requirements while retail buyers are subject to collective influences of family and friends. Strategies for addressing buyer groups must not only distinguish between types of industries but also between the characteristics of buyers of producer goods and consumer goods across developed and emerging markets. The intersection of purchasing power and buyer preference leads to a complex clustering of buyer groups.

The second principle is that every buyer has multiple needs that can be fulfilled effectively by full-line manufacturers; buyers typically need product families rather than isolated products, however unique they are. Any industrial plant, for example, would need compressors of different principles (water cooled or air cooled) and in different air pressures, based on the application. It would be inappropriate for a compressor manufacturer to specialise only in large compressors, therefore. While an airline may specialise in one type of aircraft for reasons of standardisation and nature of routes, the aircraft manufacturer has to make aircraft that suit the diverse requirements of multiple airlines. Similarly, a buyer group such as a national airports authority would require different styles and scales of baggage conveyors based on the size and build-out of the airport (metro domestic, metro international or tier 2 and tier 3 cities). Even a simple product like a writing instrument has multiple need profiles within a single buyer group; for example, low-cost ball-point pens for rough work, gel pens for official or college writing, fountain pens for signatures and premium pens for a luxury look.

Flipping the proposition

In contrast to the prescription provided by Porter of choosing buyers based on products or services available, the right proposition for a firm should be to choose its products and services based on the available buyer universe. Such a selection cannot remain static; it also cannot be based just on what is known. New as well as established companies have to constantly address the needs of seen and unseen buyers. As new companies provide new products to create new buyers, existing companies would need to debate and decide on tweaking their product offerings or developing new products to ride the consumer wave. Porter's theorems on managing buyer power would provide tactical solutions to optimise product-market fit but would be unable to provide strategic solutions for achieving sustainable growth. If we consider India's energy scene, the state electricity boards and national energy corporations in private and public sectors are clearly large buyer groups. Given the existence of several national and international power plant makers as competition, individual power plant manufacturers have little leeway to choose or leverage their buyer groups. Looking forward, all types of power plants in India, in private and public sectors, have great scope for covering a host of technologies: thermal, hydro, nuclear, solar and wind in micro, medium, large, mega and ultra-mega scales. Until buyer groups are formed, theorems of managing buyer power can make very little contribution to competitive strategy.

Perhaps the more relevant theorem in Porter's buyer power theory relates to the proposition of buyer growth. Porter rightly argues that firms should cast their lot with buyers who have greater growth potential. Buyers faced with low growth would obviously have lower budgets and would constantly seek the lowest cost products to assure themselves of some base level of cost competitiveness and profitability. Focusing on the fast-growing buyer groups, on the other hand, provides firms with scale and a degree of pricing flexibility. While the benefit of connecting with growth sectors is an obvious hypothesis, many firms fail to recognise shifting growth trends and more importantly, the need to reengineer products to meet newer growth needs. India, for example, is not merely at the cusp of an economic growth wave but also at the threshold of a major shift in consumer preferences due to changing demographics in favour of a younger population. Even companies like Apple have been late to recognise and appropriately respond to the potential of Indian buyer groups. Firms must, therefore, focus on growth direction as well as growth velocity to manage buyer power in a constructive manner.

Combating versus collaborating

Whatever the granulated merits and demerits of Porter's propositions on buyer power (which is real and cannot be ignored), the underlying idea of managing buyer dynamics to reduce buyer power is ill-advised. It is antithetical to the positive concept of the buyer being the cause and sustenance for the genesis and growth of the firm. The more appropriate proposition for the firm would be to continuously engage with buyers to serve them better. Such engagement could take several forms. At its most basic level is the trade channel utilised to approach buyers. While open display formats like the Web and multi-brand retailing are cost-effective to deploy for industrial buyers and retail consumers respectively, firms should provide distinctive user experiences for each category. Periodic connectivity through conferences and corporate sales plazas are relevant experience generators. At the most profound level, firms must be geared to co-experience with users the various life-cycle stages of the product to identify needs for product development and improvement. At an intermediate level are the classic methodologies of customer feedback, trade-channel feedback, service-centre feedback and market research, all of which provide insights to improve products and services for customers.

Positive engagement and proactive collaboration with customers or buyers provide several benefits to firms. In fact, the thesis of C K Prahalad's landmark book, *The Fortune at the Bottom of the Pyramid*, is that by understanding consumer needs and user characteristics in different economic strata, each with distinctive cultures and practices, firms can reengineer their products and open up completely new markets. The success of Japanese and Korean automobile manufacturers in India from the 1980s to 2000s was due to such a buyer-centric adaptation. Over the past few months, a new generation of European automobile makers has been targeting exclusive niche segments with their luxury car products although they do not meet the requirements of the larger resource-constrained Indian market segments. Sooner or later, this group of firms could discover the perils of playing on transient luxury buyer dynamics and not being in the group of positively engaged and socially appropriate full-line auto makers.

Employees as buyers; leaders as designers

Many firms fail to realise that their own employees are buyers too. Most firms ignore the fact that hardly any employee, save in customer-centric jobs, is provided the opportunity to interact with customers and discover how the products they make (or are associated with) fare in the hands of customers. Letting employees share their experiences of the company's and its competitors' products, and even encouraging them to buy products selectively could create useful pilot projects for understanding the more universal buyer behaviour. Market-centric behaviour can be institutionalised in companies if employees from various departments, especially R&D and manufacturing, are moved through customer-centric departments like sales, marketing, service and market research. Japanese companies are known to have deployed such an organisational strategy as a strategic tool to get institutional processes closer to customers, especially in the 1970s and 1980s when they were at the leading edge of global innovation. The Koreans mastered this in the 1990s and 2000s. Potentially, leading emerging economies such as India and China have the opportunity to make their organisations customer-integrated for enhanced competitiveness. Figure 5.1 depicts *buyer-firm relationships* that influence buyer power characteristics.

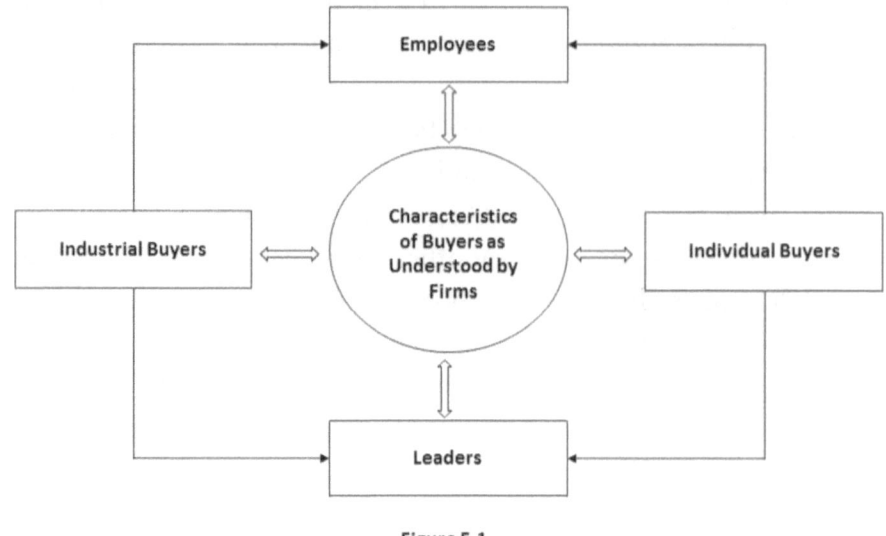

Figure 5.1
Buyer Power Characteristics

Leaders have a special role in handling buyers as a competitive force. Wise leaders would view buyers as a group that enhances the firm's competitiveness through higher expectations rather than as a group that either makes unjustified demands on company resources or shows complete tolerance of the company's offerings. Leaders tend to be more internationally and cross-culturally exposed than any other group of employees; therefore, they have a significant role in leading their corporations on the path of product innovation and customer service. Leaders are well-placed to observe, absorb and adapt latent user expectations and latest product features that are regionally relevant and/or globally available to generate creative sparks in their firms. Leaders who truly internationalise their firms on a multi-country basis (as opposed to home country-centric internationalisation) provide their firms with unprecedented opportunities to develop expansive product-market configurations. There are only a few things wise and effective leaders must focus on to lead their corporations to glory; product design and development probably ranks the highest in that list.

Buyers as corporate resource

Porter's theory suggests that buyer groups have bargaining power vis-à-vis a company, which they tend to deploy. While acknowledging this, the discussion in this chapter has pointed out that it is counterintuitive and antithetical to the genesis and growth of corporations to view buyers and companies as pitted against each other. Recognising that buyer power can be overwhelming, companies must find positive and proactive ways of engaging and integrating with customers for a better user experience rather than managing them for better sales. This provides companies both tactical and strategic wins with sustainable growth paradigms. Leadership in product development and delivery would be a core component of a company that treats customers as a genuine and fundamental corporate resource.

Chapter 6
Supplier Power and Firm Competitiveness

Supplier Power and Firm Competitiveness: Perfect Freedom versus Partnered Synergy

- As between a firm and its customers, the relationship between a firm and its suppliers needs to be more collaborative rather than competitive.
- Supplier-firm differentiation, supplier-firm connectivity, supplier-firm behaviour and supplier clusters are some of the fascinating collaborative aspects of an industry's structural evolution.
- Dual-sourcing relationships would depend on flexi-designing being an integral component of the product-development philosophy of the firm and the supplier.
- Collaboratively aligned and working together, the firm and its suppliers would achieve a more competitive presence in the marketplace for mutual benefit.

The bargaining power of suppliers is an important competitive force outlined by Michael Porter in his Five Forces Theory. As with buyer power, supplier power arises from the singular value chain, of which the firm is a part. The purchasing strategy that must be adopted by a firm to deal with supplier power has received only perfunctory treatment from Porter, relative to other competitive forces or strategies. Key purchasing and supply issues are, no doubt, treated through the analytical framework on the strategic decision of vertical integration. Such decisions are not regular occurrences, and firms must have a construct to perceptively deal with the myriad firm-supplier interfaces that occur.

In the absence of a comprehensive competitive strategy framework for supply relationships, the issues relating to supplier power are only partially addressed and that too, with the goal of buttressing a firm's competitive position. This could be due to Porter's belief that many aspects of purchasing strategy go well beyond the scope of a book on competitive strategy. However, unlike a portion of buyer groups that are individual consumers, suppliers are firms with similar value chains of buyer-supplier relationships. Competitive strategy must provide a more detailed analysis of supplier issues than Porter has provided, including his analysis of vertical integration, and even considering that supply-chain management is a different domain by itself.

Structural issues

According to Porter, there are four key issues in purchasing strategy from a structural standpoint: stability and competitiveness of the supplier pool, optimal vertical integration, allocation of purchases among qualified suppliers and creation of maximum leverage with chosen suppliers. Porter rightly hypothesises that a firm should procure from vendors who will maintain or improve their competitive position in their own industry. He recommends applying structural and competitor analysis, found throughout his work on Competitive Strategy, to ascertain how a firm's suppliers will fare on these dimensions. Porter considers vertical integration the key strategic decision in purchasing. However, this is considered contingent on identification of items for make or buy.

Porter considers a firm's allocation of purchases among its suppliers a key element in dealing with the bargaining power of suppliers. He lists the conditions that create powerful suppliers: supplier concentration, non-dependence on customers, switching costs for customers, unique or differentiated products and threat of forward integration. He advocates creating maximum leverage through diffused purchases, avoiding switching costs, qualifying alternative sources, promoting standardisation and using tapered integration. He differentiates the long-run decrease in purchasing costs through such holistic purchasing strategies from the short-run increase in costs which some strategies may entail. He concludes, as a wise purchasing manager would, that the firm should purchase from low-cost suppliers unless there are offsetting benefits in terms of long-run bargaining power. While not contradicting Porter's viewpoints, this chapter brings up several other interesting perspectives.

Division of competencies

Developing supplier-firm differentiation, supplier-firm connectivity, behavioural aspects of the supplier-firm relationship and supplier clusters are some of the fascinating aspects of an industry's structural evolution. A greater focus is needed on these aspects. Core competency in developing a component or even a whole group of components has rarely translated into core competency in developing the end-product. The essence of the historical evolution of the supplier industry as an autonomous but dependent, adjacent one to the end-product or Original Equipment Manufacturer (OEM) industry is rooted in ownership and techno-economic considerations. By theory and practice, OEMs require huge investments and mega entrepreneurship, which makes them the preserve of the few.

Component or system supplies, on the other hand, require low and mid-scale investments and provide for diffusion of entrepreneurship. Government policies also encourage the creation of larger employment opportunities through small- and medium-scale enterprises. Separating component and OEM industries helps OEMs access more cost-competitive components due to the lower direct costs and overheads of smaller enterprises. Once a component manufacturer becomes an established player, it would prefer to diversify into another component business rather than forward integrate into an OEM. At best, it may consider limited forward integration into systems manufacture. Several global and Indian component groups offer striking evidence of this focused strategic approach.

The global automobile industry is an excellent example of dichotomy as well as symbiosis between component and end-product manufacture. Over time, however, there has been greater appreciation for integrating vendors from the very early stage of new product commercialisation and ensuring seamless development of new components and end-products. In addition, the need for OEMs to have a greater say in the development of new component systems has been felt in recent times. India offers an outstanding example of an automobile component manufacturing group called TVS, which despite the established base to manufacture every conceivable automotive component (and extending even into vehicle dealerships and vehicle financing) has restrained itself from entering automobile manufacture. Rane reflects a similar trend, excelling in certain automotive components and not extending into any other facet of the automobile business.

There are two interesting perspectives to this trend. The first one is that once component makers are established as preferred vendors, they secure greater market monopoly than OEMs. For example, while the automobile manufacturing arena has several companies churning out various types of automobiles, the component making industry is a duopoly or low oligopoly. By remaining small and focused on research and manufacturing, with very little marketing investments, suppliers tend to build core competencies. From Intel chips and Samsung OLED screens to Bosch spark plugs and fuel injection equipment and ZF gear boxes, the component supplier industry structure is unmistakably concentrated. The second perspective is that being independent, yet not being visibly branded, gives suppliers complete freedom to exploit the total product market. As opposed to an industry comprising, say, thirty OEMs selling 30 million original equipment in the aggregate at an average one million end-products per manufacturer, a duopolistic component supplier industry lets the constituents enjoy an equal share each of 15 million components, probably with greater profitability than the automobile manufacturer. The division of competencies and business interests works advantageously for both the constituents, the end-product manufacturers and component vendors.

Integration of technology

Much as division of labour works to the advantage of suppliers and the firm, integration of technology should also work to their advantage. There are significant opportunities as well as limitations to technology integration. In many cases, component makers can admirably respond to firm requirements with proactive user signalling. In the automobile industry, self-cooled radiators, asbestos-free gaskets, parabolic springs, low-friction oils, tight tolerance pistons, light weight-high strength connecting rods, camshafts and crankshafts are all examples of component makers rising to technological challenges with component-level leadership. On the other hand, a few areas cannot be tackled without active and continuous collaboration. Vehicle control computers and software, external trim and external lighting, for example, need complete technological integration. Concurrent engineering could be a great way to ensure collaborative development. Yet, both OEMs and component-suppliers need to know the economics-deterrent integration level in each case. OEMs must focus on the interface and optimisation of equipment and component design, while component makers must focus on similar interfacing and optimisation with their materials suppliers.

Not surprisingly, the technological value chain of a component maker is more elaborate than the OEM value chain. Even evolved OEMs and component makers often tend to overlook such a strategic view of technology. If it were not so, tablet computers would have received more powerful and appropriate chips from Intel and more appropriate operating systems from Symbion, Android and Microsoft at first-generation launch itself. Technological integration for optimum impact tends to be a fine balance between ensuring faster go-to-market and greater proprietary confidentiality. While Porter speaks of the bargaining power of suppliers, it would appear that OEMs have significant leeway in deciding the direction and pace of component-level technologies. OEMs can retain their proactive advantage by seeking design copyrights wherever feasible or staking claim to joint intellectual property. Suppliers can secure their bargaining power in this space even while planning a more open approach by securing broad patent estates on their technologies. A good model would be for OEMs and component suppliers to dedicate a certain percentage of their development budgets to integrating component-level and OEM-level research. Such a model could lead to a better cross-fertilisation of ideas.

Collaboration of minds

As between a firm and its customers, the relationship between the firm and its suppliers needs to be more collaborative than competitive. In fact, suppliers need to have the same customer-centricity towards OEMs as OEMs need to have with their customers. Such collaboration can be successfully nurtured in two ways. One method is setting up supplier-firm steering committees to discuss field performance, customer feedback, cost competitiveness, technology vision, new product timelines, capacity plans, investment needs and so on. Such forums provide both the firm and the supplier a platform to better dovetail their strategies. If a firm is able to position itself as the complete provider of information on components, it would have better bargaining power with suppliers. The other approach is for both the firm and the supplier to, individually and collectively, reach out directly to the customer. Direct interfacing with customers provides significant additional focus on individual components and a more perceptive feedback. Larger and enlightened suppliers, in fact, prefer to secure direct feedback from the marketplace. In addition, the movement of spare parts and after-sales service metrics provide valuable feedback to suppliers. Direct feedback mechanisms can, and should, only be supplemental to the firm- and customer-level knowledge-sharing mechanisms.

Supplier power is enhanced when suppliers can access the OEMs' customers directly and understand levels of satisfaction and areas for improvement. Regardless of the methodologies adopted, it is evident that collaborative planning between the firm and its suppliers brings manifold benefits such as prompt redress of performance issues, smoother production and inventory, agility to meet market volatility, preparedness for model changes and technology upgrades and better value-chain performance and greater competitiveness. As opposed to Porter's model of short-run firm-level performance maximisation, collaboration between the firm and its suppliers enables long-run performance maximisation for both the firm and the supplier. While this is easier said than done, progressive OEMs and their vendors have traditionally sought to strengthen this approach through mechanisms such as steering committees and annual vendor meetings. Collaborative working, however, requires greater institutionalisation through processes such as collaborative forecasting, planning, capacity planning and so on. Figure 6.1 portrays a model of firm-supplier dynamics that influence supplier power characteristics.

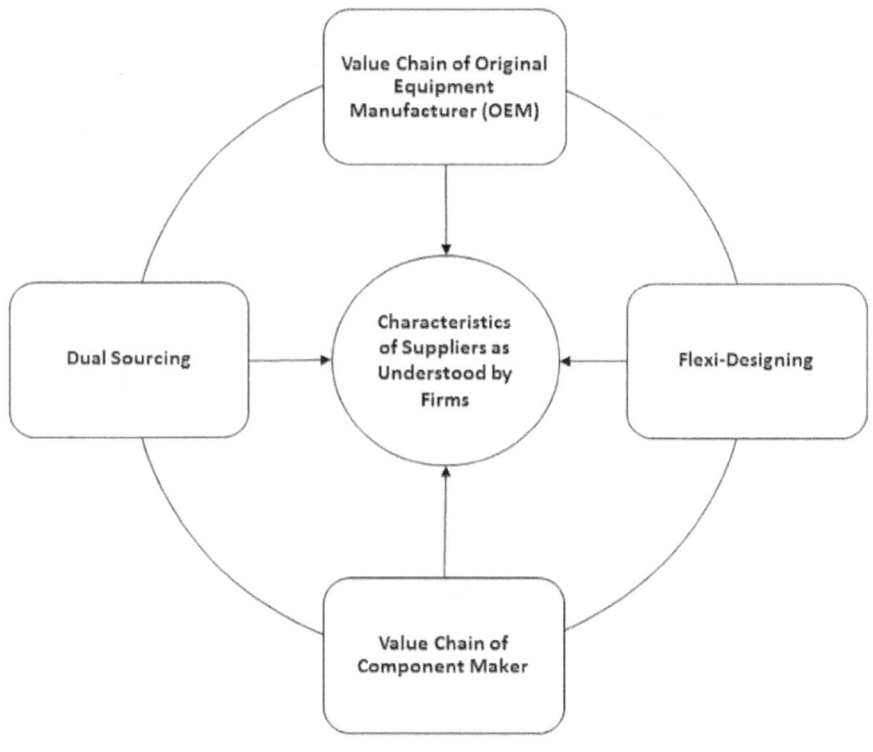

Figure 6.1
Supplier Power Characteristics

Dual sourcing and flexi-designing

The key challenge in the firm-supplier relationship is a fine balance between proprietary technology (as a market-dominating factor) and freedom to operate (as a risk-mitigating factor). Clearly, if the supplier has a unique and differentiated position, the firm would benefit from having exclusive access to supplier technology. At the same time, such exclusive dependence could lead to considerable supplier power in terms of high price or controlled delivery while the firm could face risks associated with dependence on a sole supplier, including likely disruption in the case of *force majeure* conditions affecting the supplier. To be fair, the supplier is also subject to similar risks when the firm happens to be the sole buyer. To maximise market opportunity, especially for new proprietary developments, a partnership between the firm and its vendor for strategic technologies and supplies is advisable, but dual sourcing would be an appropriate paradigm for a mutually beneficial and protective relationship.

The evolution of a dual-sourcing relationship would depend on flexi-designing being an integral component of the product-development philosophy of both the firm and the supplier. Many industries have not yet committed to standardisation of internal parts. Standardisation does not imply dilution of the differentiation advantage. A supplier of headlamps may design lamps to conform dimensionally to a standardised form factor, more particularly the fixing system, but could still achieve high differentiation in terms of lighting intensity, lighting angle, adjustments to ambient light, lamp life, cost level and so on. Industry-level standards organisations can make a significant contribution to this effort. Industries such as electrical, electronics, nuclear and pharmaceutical industries have to pre-register products and principal vendor-supplied materials with industry-level or government-level regulatory agencies. Firms in such industries must take more proactive steps to qualify alternative suppliers as part of the early product development and manufacturing processes. Flexi-designing and development helps firms to integrate alternative suppliers with low lead times for switching components and supply sources in exigencies.

Supplier power as partnership synergy

The goals of end-product manufacturers or OEMs and their suppliers are, in matter of fact, aligned. Power dynamics between the firm and its suppliers need to be harnessed in a more positive manner than articulated in the Porter model, by focusing on leveraging mutual capabilities for market competitiveness. The technological strengths of suppliers and market understanding of OEMs must be used to yield better performance of the total value chain. In the contemporary model of competitive strategy, the firm should respect the technological specialisation of its suppliers and the suppliers should respect the pressures on OEMs for higher performance and better quality at lower costs. Collaboratively aligned and working together, the firm and its suppliers would achieve a more competitive presence in the marketplace for mutual benefit.

Chapter 7
A Framework of Competitive Moves

Analysing and Developing Competitive Moves: A New Market and Practice-centric Framework

- All the players in an industry can be categorised in terms of two critical dimensions—ability to influence the market and ability to compete with other firms.
- In terms of market influence, firms in an industry tend to be one of the following: market creators, market maintainers or market destroyers.
- From the perspective of competitive advantage, firms typically fall into one of the following three categories: share builders, share maintainers and share losers.
- The nine-grid matrix correlates with revenue-profit and market size-market share markers rather well; the aspiration of firms must be to move from inferior to superior grids.

An industry comprises multiple players who together define its structural dynamics. Whether an industry is defined narrowly or broadly, it usually has at least two competitors. Monopoly is almost non-existent in current times, while duopoly exists in certain sunrise or technology-intensive industries. In most cases, however, oligopoly typifies the contemporary industry structure. As students and practitioners of management are aware, an oligopoly falls in between a monopoly, where there is only one firm in an industry, and the perfectly competitive industry, where there are several firms. Entry and growth are the most challenging in a monopolistic industry structure where competitive moves are often dictated and overwhelmed by a firm. In the perfectly competitive industry, entry is relatively easy and the competitive moves of firms are affected more by market conditions than by each other's moves. Growth, however, is tough in such an industry. In contrast, in an oligopoly, firms tend to have several entry and growth options.

In his work on Competitive Strategy, Michael Porter prescribes a framework for developing and countering competitive moves. According to Porter, in an oligopoly, a firm often faces a dilemma. It can pursue the interests (for example, profitability) of the industry as a whole (or of some subgroup of firms) and thereby not incite competitive reaction or it can behave in its own narrow self-interest at the risk of setting off retaliation and escalating industry competition to a full-scale battle. This dilemma can be resolved by choosing a balance between industry-level cooperation (to avoid profit-eroding warfare) and firm-level competition (to avoid giving up potential revenues and profits). Arguing that firms in an oligopoly are dependent on each other with respect to competitive moves, Porter outlines a series of competitive moves that firms could typically follow. He broadly classifies these as cooperative or non-threatening moves, threatening moves and defensive moves. He also hypothesises that the nature of competitive moves is influenced by industry instability (influencing the likelihood of competitive warfare) and the commitment of members to the industry (influencing the likelihood, speed and vigour of competitive moves). Porter lists several competitive options under threatening moves.

While Porter's framework of competitive moves is quite useful in developing competitive strategy, this chapter suggests an entirely different and potentially more useful framework for analysing and developing competitive moves.

Limitations of lists

Porter's approach of listing competitive moves under different heads is centred on the firm rather than the competition. The underlying theme is generic approach (a common theme throughout his work on Competitive Strategy) rather than an approach customised to the nature of competitors. For example, it talks of moves being offensive or defensive based on whether the firm is able to make its moves on a pre-emptive or responsive basis. The framework proposed by Porter is limited to functional strategies such as Timex conceptualising a different channel strategy compared to its Swiss competition. While doing so, Porter rather simplifies the competitive paradigm by suggesting that retaliatory competitive moves could be lagging by the lead time required to implement them. He suggests, for example, that responding to a long-lead competitive move such as a new automobile model or a new blast furnace would intrinsically carry a lag time. This approach is deficient in the sense that even without having perfectly competitive industry conditions, the contemporary industrial scenario is marked by perfect information. In today's world, therefore, retaliatory responses to any competitive moves could take place with a lag time of just a couple of months, which could also be overcome with better execution. Porter's theory also implies, somewhat erroneously for the current situation, that a firm's competitive move would yield a similar advantage over each competitor and that each competitor makes a similar assumption.

In addition, Porter's framework is limited by the fact that today's firms are well-anchored by continuous product improvements or yearly model changes. No firm, therefore, waits for the other firm to make a move. All the firms in an oligopolistic industry structure would be capable of undertaking competitive actions more or less simultaneously. For example, automobile makers not only undertake annual model renewals but also introduce multi-level product families (say, sub-compacts, compacts, sedans and SUVs). Computers, mobile devices and tablets have new product introductions on an almost quarterly basis. The differentiators for firms in the contemporary oligopolistic structure would, therefore, be more in terms of levels of innovation in product development, effectiveness in marketing, excellence in manufacturing and efficiency in marketplace delivery. Certain core competencies, rather than generic functional strategies, distinguish the more competitive firms from others. This hypothesis leads us to the development of an analytical framework that does not start with the categorisation and listing of competitive moves in a functionally generic methodology as suggested by Porter; rather, it crystallises a new theme that the players in the industry must first be classified on the basis of their positioning in terms of their core competencies and contingent business results. Understanding competitors in a broad typology would be an essential foundational step in analysing and defining competitive moves in the new framework.

Competitor typology

All the players in an industry can be categorised in terms of two critical dimensions: their ability to influence the market and their ability to compete with other firms. In terms of market influence, firms in an industry tend to be one of the following: market creators, market maintainers or market destroyers. The core competence of market creators lies in product innovation and creating an entirely new market through their products. Apple and Samsung constitute outstanding examples of market creators in the communication and computing devices industries. Market maintainers are competent enough to be successful product followers keeping the market live and expansive through their product followership. Most firms in an oligopolistic structure belong to this class. Companies like Lenovo are perhaps a good example of this class, both in communication and computing industries. Market destroyers are companies faced with declining competencies and unable to influence positive market development. Through their dated or dysfunctional products, market destroyers cause customers to develop a negative image of the industry. Firms that flood markets with cheap products of low functionality constitute a striking example of market destroyers. Not every industry would have firms belonging to all categories all through the years. One instance of a market-creating firm may be followed by several instances of market-maintaining firms and a few instances of market-destroying firms.

With respect to competitive advantage, firms typically fall into one of the following three categories: share builders, share maintainers and share losers. Share builders are those firms that have core competencies in marketing effectiveness, manufacturing excellence and delivery efficiency. Building on their product-development capabilities, whether of innovation or followership, such firms achieve share-building capabilities. Market creators are natural share builders as the market monopolistically develops around their innovative products. However, market creators could fail to utilise their natural share-building advantage if core competencies in any or all of the domains of marketing, manufacturing and delivery are sub-optimal. Market maintainers, on the other hand, assiduously seek to create competitive advantage as share builders to compensate for the lower level of product innovation. Share maintainers tend to be in an equilibrium state in the oligopolistic structure. Many share maintainers possess a balanced portfolio of mid-range competencies capable of maintaining a reasonable market share in an oligopolistic market. Share losers are typically uncompetitive firms, lacking any level of differentiation in product development, marketing, manufacturing and product delivery.

The firm in a nine-grid matrix

Typically, therefore, all firms in an oligopolistic industry can be categorised in various grids of the nine-grid matrix. The most competitive firm is the one which is both a market builder and a share builder while the least competitive firm is the one which is both a market destroyer and a share loser. Only a few pioneering firms fall in the most competitive grid and a few firms fall in the least competitive grid. Most firms fall in any of the remaining seven grids. The essence of the competitive moves of firms would be to move to grids that reflect a higher competitive advantage. Firms would not be able to achieve such mobility without first analysing where and how they are positioned in various grids and then developing appropriate competitive moves. Once this grid is conceptualised and effectuated in the live industrial setting, Porter's competitive strategy framework can be effectively applied. Competitive moves can be designed around core competencies required to qualify for superior grids. Similarly, each grid would have its own entry and mobility barriers, raising resource bars and adding challenge to the execution of competitive moves. The concepts of industry-level instability and firm-level commitment articulated by Porter can also be appropriately fitted on to the nine-grid matrix. Figure 7.1 depicts the nine-grid customer typology framework.

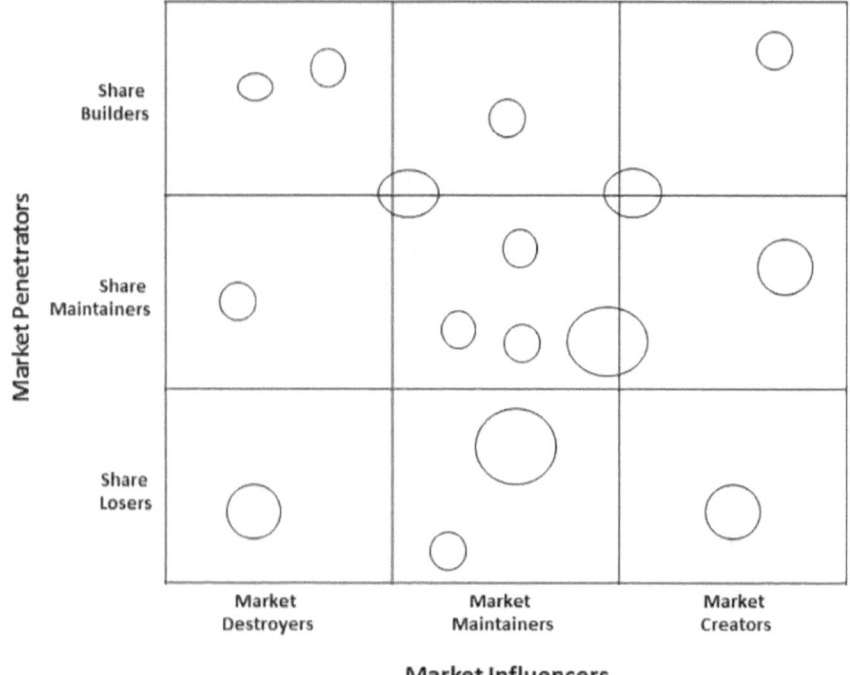

Figure 7.1
Competitor Typology

The nine-grid matrix tends to correlate rather well with revenue-profit as well as market size-market share markers. The most competitive grid corresponds to high revenue-high profit markers as much as to high manufacturing scale-high market share markers while the converse is true for the least competitive grid. Once the construct of the nine-grid matrix is recognised, it is easy to appreciate that simple defensive or offensive functional strategies would be inadequate. Tata Motors, for example, is an Indian automobile firm that is a market builder-share builder. From 1985, Tata Motors has been adding new products and new markets in the truck and bus industry, qualifying for a near permanent presence in the most competitive grid. Its principal competitor, Ashok Leyland has been a market and share maintainer, transiting in recent years into the share builder class through superior operational and market-financing strategies. Volvo, on the other hand, has been a niche player in the bus segment through its high performance, low-floor buses but has just been a share maintainer despite having product innovation (at high price). New entrants into the heavy commercial vehicle industry such as Navistar and Force Motors have been market losers as well as share losers due to an inability to develop required core competencies. Competitive moves of firms in the superior grids tend to be a combination of offensive and defensive strategies while firms in less competitive grids looking to transit to superior grids would need to follow a string of offensive strategies from model development to operational excellence, channel building and brand building.

Instability and commitment

Industry structure sets the basic parameters within which competitive moves are made by firms. Industry instability arises from evolution of technologies, processes and resources as much as from entry of new players or exit of existing players. Industry instability is a relative term in the sense that a monopolistic structure faces mild instability as it transits to a duopolistic one, which would face significant instability if it further transits to an oligopolistic structure. However, the level of instability could reduce when an oligopolistic structure transforms into a perfectly competitive one. Oligopoly offers an opportunity for competitive firms to dominate the industry, by way of a 20–80 rule (20 percent of firms dominating 80 percent of value), through appropriate competitive moves. The commitment of firms to the industry—often demonstrated by investments in technology, infrastructure, capacity and talent—has a major role to play in determining relative industry instability and relative firm stability. The lack of commitment of firms to the industry, on the other hand, leads to more share losers and eventual exits, actually consolidating and stabilising the industry in the process.

The Indian domestic airline industry offers a great example of the framework of competitive moves and the concepts of industry instability and firm commitment discussed here. Until the 1990s, the Indian domestic airline industry was the monopoly of the State-owned Indian Airlines. However, with economic liberalisation, several private airlines were allowed to enter the aviation sector, converting the industry into an oligopoly. For some years, it looked as though an industry shakeout would lead to a duopoly between Indian Airlines and Jet Airways, but after much shakeout and consolidation, eventually an oligopolistic structure emerged with different airlines being positioned differently. For example, Indigo emerged as a high-quality, low-cost market maker and share builder; Jet Airways as a share maintainer with investments in capacity, technology and talent; and SpiceJet and a few other airlines tried to be share maintainers while also being market maintainers on the plank of low cost. Interestingly, although the airline industry is highly investment and lead-time intensive, similar competitive moves (capacity expansion, aircraft modernisation, trained crew, travel safety, price competitiveness, domestic-reach extension, international routes, and electronic services) are being made by all competitors to move to superior competitive grids.

Core competencies and competitive moves

Contrary to Porter's proposition, competitive moves are not a set of functional actions or calibrated strategies that achieve superior position for firms. Competitive moves have to be based on a sub-structuring of the industry, on the dimensions of innovation and excellence, and then specifically woven around core competencies required to move from inferior competitive grids to superior ones or to defend presence in superior competitive grids. When a firm looks at itself and its competitors through the nine-grid competitor typology template, not only will its current positioning be clear but core competencies required to move to the next superior grid will also be identified. To become a market creator and a share builder requires the ultimate competencies of innovation and excellence, but there are other grids as well that benefit from select competencies and provide better-than-industry average growth and returns.

Chapter 8
Theory of Market Signalling

Porter's Theory of Market Signalling: Relevant in Contemporary Times?

- A market signal is any action by a firm that provides a direct or indirect indication of its intentions, motives, goals or internal situation; this helps in competitive strategy.
- Global economic developments are so profound that market signals are ceasing to be definitive indicators of a corporation's durable or sustainable strategy.
- Often, seemingly innocuous signals are harbingers of resolutely incredible strategies, like the Google CEO exiting the Apple Board being indicative of Google's future plans.
- Start-up companies that are hardly noticed by the general industry represent another great example of weak signals turning into strong movements.

In his work on Competitive Strategy, Michael Porter proposes that reading market signals should be considered an essential supplement to competitor analysis and an important adjunct to making effective competitive moves. According to Porter, a market signal is any action by a firm that provides a direct or indirect indication of its intentions, motives, goals or internal situation. Porter accords major emphasis to market signals despite the recognition that some are bluffs, some are warnings and only some are earnest commitments to a course of action. Porter recognises the view that given the subtlety of interpreting market signals, too much attention to them can be a counterproductive distraction. Despite this, he believes that timely recognition and accurate reading of market signals is significant to developing competitive strategy. However, like all of Porter's theories crystallised in 1980, based on research works from the 1950s to 1970s, the theory of market signalling also needs considerable refurbishing to suit the contemporary business environment.

Today, business is marked by a massive growth of information in the public domain due partly to regulatory disclosure requirements, dissemination to meet the needs of investors and analysts, information requirements of stock exchanges, governance responsibilities especially of listed companies and the competitive requirements of market making. In addition, the growth of the Internet, search engines and networking sites means that information sets on thoughts, strategies and execution of corporations are now more abundantly available than ever. Corporations are both mandatorily required and voluntarily eager to disclose as much information on their strategies and results as possible. This relative transparency is also aided by the fact that protection of intellectual property is now global, providing better protection to corporations for pre-announced product and technology moves. The massive upsurge in information also exponentially enhances the load on corporate strategy departments if they decide to start collecting and reading all market signals diligently. The role of market signals in strategy formulation clearly needs a revision.

Forms of market signals

According to Porter, market signals come in varied forms such as prior announcement of moves, announcements of results, announcements of actions after the fact, public discussions of the industry and the firm by other firms, announcements on competitive positioning and moves, discussion on tactics that could have been pursued, early implementation actions, comparisons of results and goals, cross-parry in related or unrelated areas, and fighting brands and legal actions, including public and private antitrust suits. Among these, prior announcement of moves is the most versatile form of market signalling. Purposes include capacity pre-emption, entry deterrence, threat of competitive response, setting or resetting industry-government equilibrium, test of competitor sentiment, red herrings of strategic deflection, subtle or open brand-building in the marketplace and image building among stakeholders. Today, several forums are available to send such market signals, from routine stock exchange notifications to exclusive media events.

Annual reports of firms, quarterly earnings reports and analyst and investor calls constitute the other important source of market signals, often mandated by stringent regulatory and investor requirements. Indian regulations have always had certain unique additional disclosure requirements regarding capacity, production, imports, exports, R&D, energy consumption, technology imports and assimilation and now, corporate social responsibility, all of which provide valuable signals. Indian regulations also require comprehensive management discussion and analysis of plans and results with additional information on risk management, internal controls and salary analysis in the annual reports. As firms access global markets for funds through bonds or depository receipts, comprehensive prospectuses would need to be prepared with detailed treatment of all aspects of the firm. Disclosures on environment, safety and health aspects as well as corporate social responsibility provide additional insights.

Customer-facing information undoubtedly provides the most tangible and relevant source of signal information for firms. Increasingly, firms are choosing major international conferences to showcase their developmental plans and results. In addition, regular upgrades of models and technologies, in as short timeframes as six months, is now commonplace. Technologies are openly discussed and debated as well as tested and evaluated by specialist agencies. Certification processes by industry technology bodies prior to product nomenclature provide additional valuable information. Examples are ISO, OSHA, FDA, LEED certification and so on. These certifications are not merely product or plant specific but also reflective of a firm's underlying or developing technological strength. Patent filings provide excellent insights on likely technological moves. To summarise, sources of market signals are more varied and more open than ever. The simple recognition and reading theories suggested by Porter on market signalling need to be significantly recast.

Volatility and signalling

The theory of market signalling is further vitiated by the unprecedented volatility in global economic conditions. Typically, tactics require a one-year timeline and strategy requires a timeframe of three to five years for effective execution. The economic developments in today's globalised world are so profound that market signals, however well-intentioned and robustly founded, are ceasing to be sure indicators of a corporation's durable or sustainable strategy. It is, for example, becoming impossible to predict with any degree of certainty the prices of crude, metals, commodities and agricultural products. Wild swings in the prices of basic inputs severely affect strategies built around these inputs. Market signals from industries affected by such globally volatile trends are not appropriate for any competitive analysis, except as a matter of record.

Volatility often brings in herd behaviour, which does away with the need to study individual competitive market signals and develop individual competitive moves. At times, economic volatility has a contagion effect on social attitudes and behaviour. For example, when incomes are threatened by inflation in a recessionary environment, individuals drive up demand for precious metals through hoarding rather than prudentially conserving cash. In the process, they ignore the illiquidity they are creating in their households or the potential losses they could sustain when prices soften in future. Irrational mass behaviour could extend to evolved corporations as well. For example, when recession is severe, all companies tend to be equally paranoid about cutting costs, including operational and futuristic expenses. Companies thus lose the equanimity to reassess their strategies based on their reordered internal strengths and weaknesses, external opportunities and risks. The ability to read individual market signals differently while noting overbearing economic trends is a new age requirement.

Public discussions and private inferences

Reference has been made in Porter's work as well as in this chapter to public discussions of the industry and firm-level developments in industry forums and conferences. The ability of industry-level public discussions to lead to meaningful market signalling has always been in doubt. Recent economic and political volatility has been further forcing public discussions into a format of herd behaviour. Public discussions, more often than not, serve as industry signals for public policy formulation rather than individual corporate strategy formulation. The strength of public discussions is often dependent on the extent to which various stakeholders, including governments and firms, are willing to share their experiences and perspectives in common industry forums. Figure 8.1 captures the multiple sources of market signals in an industry.

Figure 8.1
Sources of Market Signals

Market signalling through public discussions is complicated by the fact that private inferences could be quite different from public postures. In an era of escalating fuel prices, a full-line automobile manufacturer, of small fuel-efficient budget cars to large gas-guzzling luxury cars, may be as vociferous as a dedicated luxury car maker in decrying the adverse impact of galloping fuel prices. In reality, the full line manufacturer could privately be planning a major shift in product mix in favour of fuel-efficient cars. Similarly, public assurances of individual firms providing pan-industry services need to be reinterpreted based on their strategic moves. The acquisition in August 2011 by Google, which supplies open-source Android operating system to all mobile device makers, of Motorola's mobile device business pointed to a new, possibly adverse, strategic dimension for all other mobile device makers using Android operating system, notwithstanding public assurances of continued support. Although Google sold off the acquired mobile division to Lenovo in January 2014, it continued to have its Nexus series of mobile devices, and has now upped the ante in the device segment significantly with the launch of its new premium Pixel mobile phones in October 2016. The views expressed by individual firms in public forums must, therefore, be interpreted in terms of the technical and business characteristics of such firms.

Signals versus strategies

Market signals by themselves do not lead to major competitive moves. Often, companies conduct futile searches for signals when strategies are right in front of them. For example, no mobile device maker took seriously the move by Samsung to develop its novel edge display system to feature in its premium mobile devices. The move was not a veiled signal; it was a clear strategy. In today's context of intense competition, other device makers, including Apple, must surely be wondering how they ignored a clear strategy from Samsung despite the strong signal of differentiation it notified. Nokia plumping for Microsoft Windows mobile operating system was more a signal of its failing strategy than a clear amalgamation or acquisition. Thus, by recognising open strategies of competitors for intrinsic competitive position, individual firms can often derive a better understanding of the competitive landscape than a 'needle in the haystack' type of search for weak or confusing market signals.

This is not to say that signals have no relevance once a competitor's strategy becomes visible. On the other hand, signals amplify the strategy for better understanding. For example, the levels of capital commitment, manpower recruitment, product renewal, technology choices, infrastructure development and pricing competitiveness could all signify the vigour with which the strategy could be pursued. Lack of overt signals cannot, however, be taken to mean that the company has no commitment to the articulated strategy. Often, signals also reflect a recalibration of strategy to be more successful relative to experience. For example, the sale by Reliance of a fifty percent stake in its oil and gas reservoirs to BP does not indicate a reversal of strategic commitment to the oil and gas business; rather it recognises the need to be more realistic in terms of resource and technology commitments for the stability and growth of that risky business as well as of Reliance as a conglomerate overall.

Surety from subtlety

Given the contemporary emanation of market signals from multiple as well as newer and more varied sources, increased environmental volatility that dictates the fluctuating amplitude of signals, and convergence between signals and strategies, the theory of market signalling needs to be subtle and perceptive. This enables greater surety in assessment. Subtlety arises from the adoption of a three-step process: first, focusing on the strategy rather than the signals; second, evaluating the strategy in terms of external volatility and internal competencies; and third, utilising the signals to calibrate the strength of the strategy. As opposed to the scenario decades ago, it is no longer feasible or appropriate for firms to provide random signals without a well-developed strategy. Issues of materiality and corporate governance in public disclosures rule out intentional signal aberration.

Surety also emerges from the subtlety in the analysis of strategies and signals. For example, the kind of leader a firm selects to lead a new business provides a subtle but sure sign of its commitment to gaining leadership in the new business. The type of consulting organisation a firm selects to chart a new growth strategy provides a subtle but clear indicator of its commitment to develop a high-quality growth paradigm. Continuance of key growth investments, say in R&D and manpower, in times of recession provide solid evidence of a firm's desire to up the ante in the post-recession period. The technological sophistication of equipment in new projects underscores a firm's focus on quality by design. The nature of structural changes in the organisation and the pace of executive mobility in an organisation reflect the firm's willingness to be adaptive and flexible. The insights developed out of the recommended three-step process of strategy-signal analysis would be much more useful than a vanilla reading of traditional signals recommended by Porter in his 1980 work.

Innocuous signals and incredible strategies

Often, seemingly innocuous signals are harbingers of resolutely incredible strategies. The exit of the chief executive of Google from the board of directors of Apple in August 2009 was a clear indicator of Google's strategy to enter the cellular communication and computing arena, fortified further by its acquisition of the Android entity. Similarly, the company's strategy to make a Google phone, Nexus, was also indicative of its desire to enter the mobile device space, later established in no uncertain manner by the acquisition of Motorola's mobile device business (though later divested to Lenovo), and the recent launch of high-end Pixel premium phones. Strategists must brood on even seemingly innocuous signals for their implicit strategic intent. Samsung's entry into the biologics business is both a confusing signal and a measured strategy. It probably needs more than hard analytics to identify which one-off signals are clear indicators of incipient moves backed by immaculate and resolute strategies.

Start-up companies are hardly noticed by the general industry. They represent another great example of weak signals turning into strong movements. Often, major firms are so preoccupied with the analysis of their peers that they fail to notice the major shifts in industrial structure resulting from the pioneering technologies and businesses that start-ups pursue. The growth or imminent growth of application or new platform developers in the mobile space into large firms in the digital industry is an indicator of how signals could be missed. A day might even come when Apple, Facebook, Google and Microsoft regret the missed opportunity of developing their own bolt-on applications and establishing new platform divisions and make up for the missed opportunity through expensive acquisitions. Reading subtle signals that are actually sound strategies requires an intuitive flair as much as it does analytical skill!

Chapter 9
Competitor Clusters and Competitor Analysis

Competitor Clusters: A Framework for Competitor Analysis

- Porter's methodology requires that the firm, especially its strategy department, train its telescope on what happens in the external marketplace.
- This book proposes an inside-out approach of organisations equipping themselves with adequate knowledge of industry-shaping trends or inputs on competitive trends.
- Competitive forces vary in their intensity and volatility depending upon how firms and strategic groups deploy their competitive capabilities.
- Focus on competitive clusters would guide the firm to the essential competencies that enable a superior competitive advantage.

Michael Porter's work on Competitive Strategy follows up the building blocks of structural analysis and generic competitive strategies with a framework for analysing competitors. Porter holds that an in-depth analysis of competitors, using the format he prescribes, provides a better perspective for formulating a firm's competitive strategy. He believes that most firms conduct a perfunctory competitor analysis, resulting in deficient strategies. He observes that many companies do not collect information about competitors systematically, but act on informal titbits of information making the competitor analysis desultory.

The framework for competitor analysis proposed by Porter comprises four diagnostic components: future goals, current strategy, assumptions and capabilities. However, he advocates an extensive canvas of study, covering data from the parent corporation's vision and group strategy to the goals and execution plans of individual business units. Porter lays out a comprehensive database, comprising over 100 markers and metrics, to identify competitor profiles. Although Porter's hypothesis and framework for competitor analysis are interesting—and as he recommends, can be applied for self-analysis too—there are conceptual and practical weaknesses in the model. This chapter addresses some of these.

Challenges of Porter's framework

The theory of competition is challenging since there can be no single definition of competition or competitor. Firstly, it is linked to the industry definition, which is in itself a moving target in the contemporary business environment given the rapid changes in product profiles and market dynamics (industry definition is discussed in Chapter 11). Secondly, competitors could have individual businesses that compete differently in diverse product-market combinations. The more a corporation is unitised and globalised, the greater the chance of multiple styles of competition from the same company. It goes without saying that the competitive profile of a single business firm and that of a business within a conglomerate could be completely different.

Porter throws in an important dimension when he hypothesises that the study of competition should cover both current and emerging competitors. However, he does not indicate whether such a study must include all competitors, a cross-section of them or only the top two or three. There could be two views on this, both with their own valid points. On the one hand, it might be sufficient if the best of competition is benchmarked for superior performance. On the other hand, even a trivial competitor could destroy an industry structure by taking irrational actions that generate intense competitive forces. This suggests that a comprehensive and insightful competitor analysis could be not only complex but also resource-intensive.

Outside-in versus inside-out

From a process point of view, Porter's methodology requires that the firm, especially its strategy department, train its telescope on what happens in the external marketplace. From a range of data including published industry statistics, competitive signals, supplier deliveries and equipment orders, the firm is expected to systematically receive inputs that define the strategies of competitors. Obviously, while this might be achievable in duopolistic and reasonably oligopolistic industry structures, it could be an impossibly people-intensive task in fragmented industries and a proprietary process in knowledge industries. Porter himself admits the challenges in reliable collection of data on competitors.

Contrary to Porter's classic outside-in approach, the inside-out approach takes the view that large organisations and innovative firms would have adequate knowledge of industry-shaping trends or inputs on competitive trends from employees who joined the firm from other competitors. The inside-out approach thus does not differentiate internal firm developments from competitive external developments. As a result, no specific resources are allocated for dedicated external competitive intelligence in the inside-out approach. Self-analysis and competitor analysis converge in terms of process mechanics. Firms following the inside-out approach encourage their employees to actively interact with the outside world, including participation in local and global industry events.

Strategic groups

Clearly, neither the outside-in nor the inside-out approach helps in establishing a robust and sustainable framework of competitor analysis that has a fair balance of resource deployment and information collection. When scores of competitors are analysed over several dimensions, each with multiple metrics, the emerging picture would be too diffused to provide any meaningful conclusions. It would be more relevant to study convergent patterns of collective competitive behaviour than divergent profiles of individual competitive behaviour at the firm level. The theory of strategic groups discussed in Chapter 4 offers interesting insights in this context. As discussed earlier, strategic groups comprise firms following the same or a similar strategy, in each case, along strategic dimensions. These could be dimensions such as specialisation and integration.

I tested the relevance and appropriateness of strategic groups in industry analysis through research studies conducted at the Indian Institute of Technology Madras, with the Indian automobile industry as the background. Dimensions such as import dependence, export competitiveness, product diversity and R&D intensity emerged as useful criteria to develop strategic groups and predict their performance. However, strategic groups do not qualify to be used as the basis for analysing competitive behaviour. Adoption of a particular strategy, and even its execution, merely indicates competitive intent; it does not necessarily reflect competitive behaviour or competitive outcome. Competitive forces vary in intensity and volatility depending upon how firms and strategic groups deploy their competitive capabilities. Strategic groups with an overlay of competitive behaviour could provide a simpler yet a more effective approach to analyse competition. Figure 9.1 relates strategic strengths and competitive behaviours of firms in a typical format.

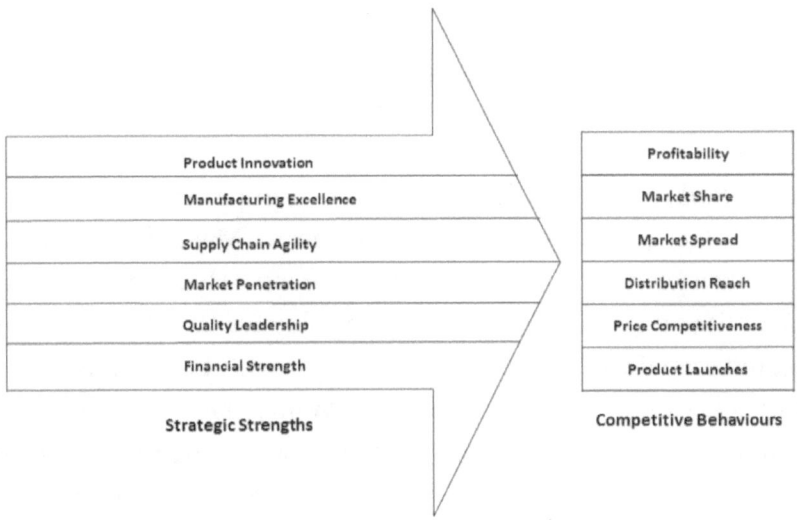

Figure 9.1
Strategic Strengths and Competitive Behaviours

Competitor clusters

Competitor clusters can be defined as strategic groups that deploy their competencies with a differential competitive intensity. A group that is R&D intensive could be low on the competitive use of such innovative intensity. Indian power plant producers as a strategic group are as innovative and cost efficient as Chinese ones. However, the latter are far more aggressive in leveraging their national systemic cost-competitiveness to gain a lead over Indian power plant producers. Clearly, while formulating its competitive strategy, an Indian power plant producer would need to look at a different competitor cluster than it is used to. The paradox of competitor clusters is evident from the low-cost mobile phone market. Korean (Samsung and LG) and Swedish (Sony Ericsson and Nokia) mobile device leaders had ultra-low cost devices just as the Indian (Micromax) and Chinese (Huawei) device makers have. However, the latter's approach to translate their low-cost position into ultra-low price position, with additional smart phone features, positions them in a different (and superior) competitor cluster.

A review of the Indian automobile industry provides an additional example of competitor clustering. The industry comprises a fascinating array of companies with different strategic attributes: a wholly multi-line indigenous company (Tata Motors), a wholly indigenous specialised company (Ashok Leyland), a largely indigenised company (Maruti-Suzuki), and different strategic groups of companies with American (General Motors, Ford), European (Mercedes Benz, BMW, Audi, Volkswagen, Fiat and Renault), Korean (Hyundai) or Japanese (Toyota, Nissan, Honda and Isuzu) technologies. Within each strategic group are strategic sub-groups of companies with high levels of import dependence and/or luxury orientation. While these companies could be grouped on the basis of technological and business strategies as above, different competitor clusters would emerge when the competitive behaviour profiles are superimposed. A firm planning to enter the Indian automobile industry space needs to be conscious of not only the strategic group it could form a part of but also the competitor cluster it would need to contend with.

Dimensions for clustering

Firms could pursue several strategic dimensions but not all of these are relevant for strategic grouping or even appropriate for competitor clustering. Strategic strengths essentially are reflected in terms of product innovation, manufacturing excellence, supply-chain agility, market penetration, quality leadership and financial strength. Competitive behaviour is reflected in the pace of product launches, price competitiveness, distribution reach, market spread, market share and profitability. A combination of strategic strengths and competitive behaviour would help develop relevant competitor clusters. While there could be thirty-six combinations of strategic strengths and competitive behaviours, only a few are significant for competitor clustering. Relevant combinations are those that are more inversely correlated than others.

The essence of competitive excellence lies in the ability to pursue strategies that are apparently contrarian but are equally result oriented. One facet of competitive intensity is an ability to consume significantly high levels of resources (for example, an unceasing introduction of successive generations of products) and yet achieve outcomes that provide significantly high levels of financial strength (for example, high levels of product profitability). Another facet of competitive strength is an ability to pack maximal innovation into minimal product count (for example, just one or two products per year, each packed with breakthrough features) and still achieve maximal market spread and market share (for example, global market footprint and over fifty percent market share). Yet another facet could be an ability to have the widest possible distribution capability with the lowest product pricing (for example, mass retailing of budget products) and still achieve high levels of financial strength (for example, corporate profitability). Toyota, Apple and Walmart are institutional examples of the three facets of competitive profiling, respectively.

Competitive clustering can be conducted in terms of simple integrated hypotheses as above (for example, most profitable innovation) or could be developed in terms of high-low 2×2 grids. In this approach, firms would be classified on appropriate scales in terms of innovation intensity and product profitability to develop four grids. Figure 9.2 illustrates.

	Innovation Intensity Low	Innovation Intensity High
Product Profitability High	Tactically Superior Competitors	Strategically Outstanding Competitors
Product Profitability Low	Operationally Weak Competitors	Tactically Superior Competitors

Figure 9.2
A Simple Competitor Cluster

The grids represent clusters that are high on both innovation and profitability, high on either innovation or profitability on the one hand and correspondingly low on either profitability or innovation on the other, and low on both innovation and profitability. Greater clarity would be achieved by adopting the grid approach to develop competitive clusters of firms. By adopting the scaling technique, multiple competitive clusters could be positioned in a rather representative manner in each of the four grids.

Guidance for entry

Any strategic framework should help firms achieve successful entry into or growth in an existing industry. The strategic formulations for entry and growth are, however, different. A new entrant to the industry must decide fundamentally on the strategic group to choose the right positioning within the industry, consistent with available or accessible resources. For example, for a new entrant to the white goods industry, depending on the nature of product and manufacturing technologies as well as market plans and financial resources, it would be necessary to decide whether the company should join a full-line, vertically integrated strategic group or a narrow-line, outsourcing strategic group. Alternatively, a new entrant to the Indian automobile industry, depending on ownership strength and resource allocation to the region, must decide whether it would be a part of the import-dependent luxury car strategic group or a part of the indigenous component-based low and mid-range sedan strategic group.

Choice of a strategic group provides an appropriate strategic focus and scope to a new entrant. That alone does not, however, assure success. It becomes necessary to understand how the appropriate competitor cluster would respond to the new entrant. When Nissan decided to enter the Indian automobile industry, it chose the mass-market oriented small car strategic group but decided to benchmark itself against the luxury-oriented competitor cluster. Nissan sought differentiation through upgraded features, modern manufacturing and niche marketing. In contrast, Volkswagen chose the import-dependent, luxury car strategic group but positioned itself on a competitor cluster that offers a wider range of automobile models with higher levels of technology. For new entrants as well as established firms repositioning themselves, the choice of an appropriate strategic group is as important as the choice of competitor cluster, in each case.

Guidance for growth

Each firm in an industry, by virtue of evolution, falls into one or another strategic group. The successful growth of an existing firm in an established industry depends on analysis of competitors and development of appropriate strategic responses. Such strategic reconfiguration could potentially move the firm into a different strategic group. Strategic reconfiguration by several firms could also lead to the formation of new strategic groups with different characteristics. An existing firm, therefore, needs to focus on an appropriate competitor cluster and overcome competitive forces. Focus on competitive clusters would guide the firm onto the essential competencies that enable superior competitive advantage. Reverting to the case of the Indian automobile industry, the growth and the continued dominance of Maruti-Suzuki is attributable to the company recognising appropriate competitor clusters and responding to them. Maruti has fought back competitor moves by successfully extending its presence to more strategic groups (from small car to sedan car, utility vehicle and crossovers). On the other hand, the modest growth of other car manufacturers with American and European technologies is attributable to their being focused on strategic group membership rather than benchmarking themselves with competitor clusters.

An existing firm has the advantage of incumbency, since not all strategies need to be developed and executed from a zero base. It also has, as a corollary, the disadvantage of the legacy of certain ineffective strategies that could have been pursued in the past. Overriding such advantages and disadvantages, existing firms can, through the competitive cluster framework, realise a unique potential to identify winning strategies to achieve industry leadership. Rather than get lost in a laundry list of all competitive parameters of all players, a firm should simply focus on the essentials of competitive strategies of competitive clusters. A range of six dimensions (sufficient in most cases) to thirty-six strategic dimensions (that may be required in highly fragmented industries) and a 2×2 matrix of the most critical dimensions as discussed in this chapter would be required in a comprehensive competitive cluster framework. The competitive forces that exist in an industry are a cause as well as a result of the various actions taken by incumbent and new firms. Rather than follow a unit-level, multi-factor competitor analysis as proposed by Porter, this chapter suggests a more efficient and more effective competitor cluster framework, which works extremely well with a selective additional deployment of the framework of strategic groups. Competitive clustering is more dynamic than strategic grouping and provides more perceptive and more impactful dimensioning for firms to understand and respond to competitors' strategic behaviour in an industry and optimise a firm's potential.

Chapter 10
Competitive Strategy and Competitor Analysis

Generic Competitive Strategy and Specific Competitive Advantage: Viable Paradigm or Visible Paradox?

- In the past, the traditional product life cycle had a relatively high longevity; today, technology is fast-paced, products are multi-functional and life cycles are much shorter.
- Deploying technology and talent such that multiple industries are brought under one roof provides a more enhanced value proposition to the user.
- Firms can be categorised into four grids, based on a matrix of cost leadership and product differentiation, each providing relevant value propositions.
- The greater the proportion of firms with both differentiation and cost leadership, the greater the prospect of a high-growth industry that transforms society.

Unlike scientists and technologists who tend to grapple with ever-increasing complexity to develop new products, managers and leaders typically look for simple and standard prescriptions to navigate the business environment. Whether it is the BCG Matrix or McKinsey 3 Business Horizons, simplicity is offered as the best way to script a future path. Understanding the firm in the context of an industry through an expansive listing of competitive factors and forces has been the foundation of Porter's work on Competitive Strategy, first formulated in 1980. The previous chapters of this book have focused on specific aspects of Porter's Competitive Strategy, recapping relevant hypotheses and outlining refurbishments and refinements to cater to current and emerging times.

This chapter focuses on another important facet, namely generic competitive strategies. The word generic reflects the universal nature of application of these strategies rather than the level of innovation or rather the lack of it. More than structural analysis, Porter's articulation of the three simple generic competitive strategies to aid in a firm's strategy formulation and superior performance has found favour with strategists and leaders. Porter notes that the best strategy for a firm is ultimately a unique construction reflecting its particular circumstances. His advocacy as well as followers' loyalty has been to the elegant macro approach of the three generic strategies. This chapter questions the infallibility and appropriateness of the rather simplistic approach rooted in the days of simpler industrial competition and slower technological change.

Three generic strategies

According to Porter, at the broadest level, firms can identify three internally consistent generic strategies (which can be used singly or in combination) to create a defendable position in the long run and outperform competitors in an industry: overall cost leadership, differentiation and focus. Porter holds that sometimes a firm can successfully pursue more than one approach as its primary target, although he also feels that this possibility would be rare. According to him, implementing any of these generic strategies usually requires total commitment, and supporting organisational arrangements could be diluted if there is more than one primary target. The returns that a firm can reap by pursuing any of the three strategies could range from 'acceptable' to 'high,' depending on the nature of the industry. Figure 10.1 illustrates the mix of the three strategies.

82 ◂◂ Competitive Strategy

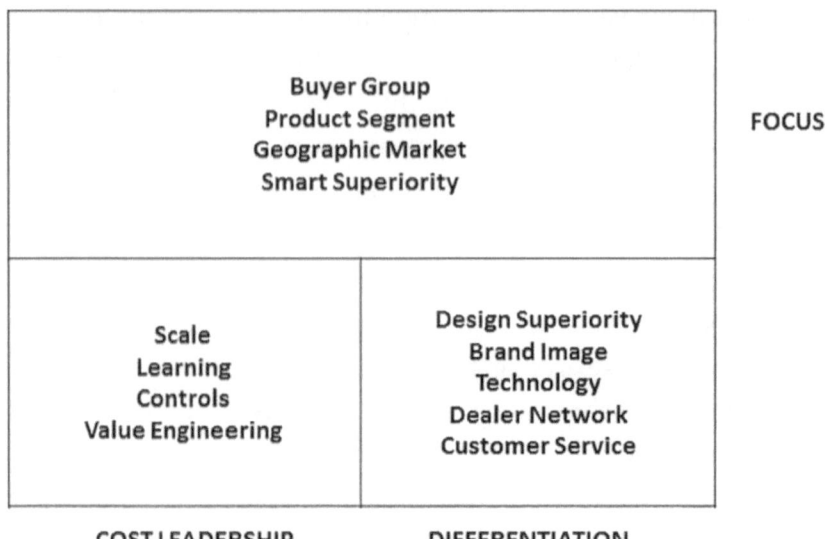

Figure 10.1
Porter's Generic Competitive Strategies

Porter hypothesises that the competitive strategies are unique as each of them requires a different set of functional policies. For example, he considers that cost leadership requires aggressive construction of efficient scale facilities; vigorous pursuit of cost reduction from experience; tight cost and overhead control; avoidance of marginal customer accounts and cost minimisation in functions such as R&D, service, sales force, advertising and so on. A great deal of managerial attention to cost control is necessary to achieve these aims. Low cost relative to competitors becomes the theme running through the entire strategy, although quality, service and other areas cannot be ignored. Cost leadership usually provides the firm above-average returns; a cost leader is usually the last to exit a declining industry. Cost leadership is held to require high relative market share.

In contrast, differentiation requires a different set of functional policies, according to Porter. These are: design or brand image, technology, features, customer service, dealer network or other dimensions, with the firm usually differentiating across multiple dimensions. Differentiation earns for the firm above average to high margins but Porter postulates that it often requires dilution of market share and cost objectives. Porter proposes focus as a third generic strategy that creates specific strategies around serving a chosen target, such as a buyer group, product segment or geographic market, particularly well. All functional strategies are developed around serving the target. The focus strategy enables above-average returns and involves a trade-off between profitability and sales volume while it may or may not involve a trade-off with overall cost position.

According to Porter, the three generic strategies are alternative, viable approaches to dealing with competitive forces. A firm failing to develop its strategy in at least one of the three directions is considered 'stuck in the middle.' Such a firm is said to lack the market share, capital investment and resolve to play the low-cost game, the industry-wide differentiation necessary to obviate the need for a low-cost position or the focus to create differentiation or a low-cost position in a more limited sphere. It is almost guaranteed low profitability. Porter believes that such a firm must make a fundamental strategic decision to adopt one of the three generic strategies but almost inevitably faces an uphill task in ascertaining which generic strategy marks the best shift and marshalling the resources for that.

Universal and non-proprietary

The goal of all firms is to grow. Growth can be achieved only through competitive advantage. According to Porter and various others, competitive advantage is the ability of a firm to utilise its attributes and resources such that it has a superior and sustainable position in the industry or market relative to its competitors. The thrust of Porter's competitive strategy framework is that the three generic strategies provide the firm with a strategic approach to gain competitive advantage. The paradox, however, is that any knowledge available at a generic level and accessible by every firm hardly provides the wherewithal to generate a firm-specific competitive advantage. In today's competitive world, any industry or market is typically composed of several players, many of them well-endowed with resources and capabilities. To assume, as

Porter does, that firms can easily achieve competitive advantage through the pursuit of any of the three generic competitive strategies is somewhat simplistic.

Commoditisation of not merely products and services but even of underlying technologies is a modern development that reflects low entry barriers and high competition in mature or declining industries and markets. The same applies to strategy formulation too. Commodity-like marketing of simplistic strategic prescriptions would make good reading but could spell bad business. The underlying determinants of competitive strategy are not simple and superficial factors like scale and features; rather, they are the complex and embedded competencies such as technology and talent. The transformation of generic competitive strategies into firm-specific competitive advantage can occur only through integration of technology and talent in strategy formulation. Technology and talent would be the tools to go beyond Porter's high-level and 'either-or' approaches of generic competitive strategies.

Technology and talent

In the past, the traditional product life cycle had higher longevity because the pace of innovation was slow, consumer tastes were stable, brand loyalties were steady, switching costs were high and industry rivalry was comfortable. Today, technology is fast paced, not only because of high R&D expenditure aimed at both incremental and breakthrough innovations but also because several base technologies are continuously being developed to be licensed and integrated with product technologies. This coupled with multi-functionality of products provides a great bandwidth for firms to attempt differentiation like never before. The central themes of a sustainable strategy for a contemporary firm are innovation and differentiation rather than scale and cost.

This does not mean that scale and cost are not important; actually, they go hand-in-hand with innovation and differentiation. In fact, the challenge is to harness technology and talent such that in spite of a shortening product life cycle and a lengthening investment cycle, it deploys the best technology and talent, which obviously come with high costs, to achieve high levels of differentiation and low levels of cost. From a technology point of view, two streams of development are to be mandatorily followed. The first is a seamless upgrade of product and process technologies on a continuous basis to provide the benefits of continuous incremental innovation at the lowest incremental investments. This must occur annually, and in some cases, even on a six-monthly basis. The second is a breakthrough transformation of product and process technologies to take the products to an entirely new platform. This must occur at least every two or three years, and in some cases even on an annual basis.

The consequent demands on talent management are many, as the contributions of a properly attuned talent base for such a technological approach could be manifold. By focusing on high levels of accomplishment in academic and industrial careers and by providing a development environment that enables innovative thinking, firms can institutionalise technological innovation in day-to-day and strategic operations. This requires, at times, obtaining solutions from domains beyond the core field. One of the reasons for a spurt in insulin usage, for instance, goes beyond the recognition of the benefits of an early start of an insulin regime or development of long-acting insulin types. It relates, in fact, to the reduction in the pain and discomfort caused to the patient while administering injections by developing shorter, thinner and less painful insulin needles, thus lowering the barrier to enhanced usage of insulin.

Extending the analogy further, the development of easy-to-carry, and easy-to-administer insulin pens, with insulin that does not require refrigerated storage, has expanded the scope for insulin even more. Clearly, an innovative product combined with innovative delivery adds to product differentiation and enhances overall product acceptance. The attendant benefit of higher scale easily overcomes the underlying need for higher investments for innovative products and delivery systems. The challenge, therefore, is one of deploying technology and talent to bring multiple industries under one roof and provide users an enhanced value proposition. Multi-disciplinary research, tie-ups with different divisions of universities and research institutions and an open approach to technology licensing are required to achieve such a transformational amalgam of technology and talent.

Cost leadership-differentiation matrix

The above discussion not only negates Porter's singular generic competitive strategy model but also reinforces the need for a new paradigm that fuses both cost leadership and product differentiation approaches. Fundamentally, the new paradigm considers cost leadership occurring not in terms of singular price-competitiveness numbers but in terms of broad cost bands. This approach allows firms to be categorised as leaders or followers on the cost dimension. Similarly, product differentiation is seen in terms of transformational or incremental innovation, enabling firms to be categorised similarly on the product differentiation front. Firms can then be slotted into four categories, each providing relevant value propositions. Figure 10.2 provides a snapshot of the cost leadership-differentiation matrix.

Figure 10.2
Cost Leadership-Differentiation Matrix

A differentiation and cost leader achieves high market share rapidly and enters a virtuous cycle of share and scale, feeding more research and innovation. Such a firm truly masters the strategy of mass customisation or the enviable task of offering the most differentiated product to the largest base of consumers. Apple is a classic example. A differentiation leader but a cost follower is a niche player with low share and scale but high acceptability. Jaguar and Rolls Royce fall in this category. A cost leader but a differentiation follower would usually start with an initial advantage of scale but would quickly find that the intrinsic inability to reap above-average returns severely limits its ability to invest in research for innovation. Many firms in emerging markets and late starters in advanced markets fall in this bracket, mimicking technology trends through technological followership. The fourth cluster of firms are differentiation and cost followers; they tend to have low capability for achieving any type of competitive advantage. Firms specialising in commodity and generic products, whether in advanced or emerging markets, exemplify this non-value adding cluster.

Each of the four clusters described above has a bearing on industry evolution. The greater the proportion of firms with both differentiation and cost leadership, the greater the prospect of the development of a high-growth industry that transforms society. The greater the proportion of firms with differentiation leadership and cost followership, the greater the propensity for a sunrise industry. The greater the proportion of firms with cost leadership and differentiation followership, the greater the likelihood of the industry turning mature and needing the impetus of transformational inputs. The greater the proportion of firms with cost and differentiation followership, the greater the risk of a terminally declining industry. Sunrise industries can become high-growth industries by mastering cost leadership, but mature industries would need to reinvent themselves on both cost leadership and differentiation to prevent slippage into a stage of terminal decline.

From generic to specific

As the discussion above demonstrates, Porter's generic competitive strategy framework—simple, elegant and popular though it is—has probably ceased to be relevant in today's era of fast-changing technologies, user needs and global shifts. An ability to integrate the dimensions of cost leadership and product differentiation under a harmonised competitive strategy framework driven by technology and talent is essential for the contemporary firm. Such an integrated competitive strategy would not only provide sustainable competitive advantage for a firm but also determine a more fundamental and epochal industry evolution.

Chapter II
Structural Analysis and Industry Definition

Structural Analysis and Industry Definition: Moving Targets in an Evolving Environment?

- Digital technologies are reshaping industries in four ways: reinforcement, reconfiguration, transformation and reinvention.
- Reinforcement makes existing products better through digital technologies. Reconfiguration readjusts both digital and brick-and-mortar businesses to complement their operations.
- Transformation happens when digital technologies create an entirely new domain of applications for products and services. Reinvention is the next horizon of artificial intelligence, machine learning and robotics.
- Each of these industry changes has a different impact on each of the five industry-level competitive forces that are a part of Porter's theory.

The structural analysis framework and the definition of industry are central to Michael Porter's landmark works on Competitive Strategy (1980) and Competitive Advantage (1985). According to Porter, industry structure has a strong influence in determining the competitive rules of the game and the strategies potentially available to a firm. Since forces outside the industry usually affect all firms in the industry, the different abilities of firms to deal with them are critical. In this context, Porter proposes the five forces that drive industry competition as bargaining power of suppliers, bargaining power of buyers, threat of substitute products or services, threat of new entrants and rivalry among existing firms. He hypothesises that collectively these five forces determine competition in an industry. He posits that each competitive force has multiple structural determinants. In earlier chapters, we have discussed how economic forces have become overarching competitive forces and developed new models. For the purposes of this chapter, however, we will limit the discussion to Porter's basic industry-level competitive forces.

Despite its centrality in his argument, industry definition is accorded a lower scale of importance by Porter. He adopts the working definition of an industry as a group of firms making products that are close substitutes for each other. He also observes that a great deal of attention has been paid to defining the relevant industry as a crucial step in competitive strategy formulation and that the proper definition of the industry or industries has become an endlessly debated subject. Porter proposes that structural analysis, by focusing broadly on competition well beyond existing rivals, should reduce the need for debates on where to draw industry boundaries. He even suggests that industry definition has little to do with the choice of strategy. Porter holds that industry definition is not the same as defining where the firm wants to compete, that is, defining its business. He advocates that decoupling industry definition and defining a firm's businesses will go a long way in eliminating needless confusion in drawing industry boundaries. While it is expedient to define business as a multi-industry concept, a stronger foundation would emerge when a dynamic concept of industry is also established as the underlying basis.

Porter's paradox

Porter's interesting hypothesis ignores the fact that, irrespective of firm-level business definition, industry would remain the operating concept influencing a nation's policy environment and a firm's competitive strategy. Structural analysis is rooted in the industry, the definition of which is not rooted in any particular methodology. By providing considerable freedom for firms to draw boundaries, Porter ensures that firms that apparently view themselves as part of an industry are, in fact, more realistically parts of different industries. This paradox is visible in multi-product industries such as the automobile industry where each product group—trucks, buses, cars, three-wheelers, two-wheelers and tractors—could be considered a separate industry since different types of customers use these products. The industry has broad-factor commonalities such as four-wheeler cars and two-wheeler motorcycles and scooters, all of which cater to personal and family transportation. Strategy formulation is expected to be based on structural analysis, which is itself allowed to be based on multiple industry and market segments.

The paradox of industry definition becomes sharper if one takes into account the fast-changing technological developments that are constantly redrawing product profiles, specifications and usage factors. Earlier, different methods of communication such as voice, data, print and visual used to have discrete products and services. Today, convergent products provide divergent services while the same service can be provided by different products. Industry segments and market segments appear to follow no particular pattern. At another level, the distinction between a product and its service has blurred, and the symbiosis between a product and its applications has increased enormously. The application of structural analysis, therefore, seems imperfect whichever the canvas chosen to define the industry. There is a case for redrawing the parameters of structural analysis and industry definition in the current era, given over three decades of profound technological changes.

Industrial digitisation

Over the past three decades, every industry has been reshaped by electronics and software as a broad stream of digital technologies, exemplified by computing, communication, navigation and sensing technologies, among others. The intensity and scope of this reshaping occurs in four ways: reinforcement, reconfiguration, transformation and reinvention. Reinforced industries are those that retain their basic technological characteristics and usage requirements but have deployed digital technologies to redefine levels of sophistication. Transformed industries have been almost threatened to extinction by digital technologies but have altered themselves through integration of digital technologies. Reinvented industries have created totally new products and services to fulfil basic requirements, some of which have been discovered out of their latency. A few examples in each case demonstrate the complexity of structural analysis and industry definition in the emerging scenario.

Reinforcement

Most basic and core industries have been substantially reinforced by the integration of electronics. Digital technologies that achieve sharper levels of measuring, computing and control have reinforced most products in basic industries to new levels of perfection. Thus, while a car remains a car, it bears little resemblance to older models in terms of functionality, from fuel combustion to cruise control and seating comfort to driving safety. The future car with autonomous driving could be entirely different. The structural factors that defined industry competition in Porter's model are no longer valid in their entirety. There are new factors of integration and differentiation through digital technologies that influence structural analysis and industry definition in several basic industries covering steel, engineering, mining, automobiles, housing, oil, aerospace and transportation, to quote a few.

Reconfiguration

Several industries in the consumer sector, on the other hand, were initially threatened by the emergence of digital technologies that promised to provide completely new ways to design, manufacture and deliver products and services to consumers. Internet changed the way producers and consumers were connected. Electronic retailing made brick-and-mortar retailing feel highly threatened. Digital imaging made film photography obsolete. Electronic books offered a new channel for book procurement and reading, closing down physical book stores. Eventually, however, conversion of digital threats into business supplements enabled several industries to recover and transform themselves. Retail, publishing, imaging, measuring, diagnostic and several media and entertainment businesses, to quote a few, have reconfigured themselves to have both parallel and integrated physical and electronic business segments. At the same time, digital retailers have also understood the importance of brick and mortar in terms of product, warehousing and distribution support.

Transformation

Connectivity has emerged as a new industry that not only spanned many existing industries but also created new industry and market segments. Bringing together advances in telecommunications, electronics and software, connectivity became a customer-centric, technology-driven platform for a new wave of multiple industries and multiple businesses. Information search, data analytics, social networking and convergent communication have created new products and services and an entirely new domain of applications for products and services. As a result, a new mega industry of conglomerate convergence has emerged, driven by software and hardware behemoths like Microsoft, Google, Apple and Facebook. Models of structural analysis and industry definition need total reconstruction to cater to the reinvented mega industries of the networking era.

Reinvention

The next horizon is clearly the deployment of artificial intelligence, machine learning and robotics to create completely new products and services. It is not inconceivable that in the future, the world could be dominated by this new package of digital technologies. An ambulatory sentry robot that has night vision, imaging, recording and replay capability, can talk to residents and police in case of housebreaks and can raise alarms is a near-term possibility. Automation of coding and testing of codes is another possibility. Automation of routine software codes is also a possibility. Home and hospital bedside help by robots is also on the cards. On the one hand, the Internet of Things would connect all devices and on the other, each industry or a set of industries would have artificial intelligence products enabling different ways of human living and other collaterals like pet caring, crop tending or animal protection.

Structural determinants

Structural analysis aims to identify the basic, underlying characteristics of an industry, rooted in its economics and technology, that shape the arena in which the competitive strategy of a constituent firm must be set. The basic framework of Five Forces structural analysis, which comprises the forces of entry, rivalry, substitutes, buyers and suppliers, remains valid with respect to the four industrial typologies discussed above. However, the structural determinants vary significantly as a group when compared to the classic Porter delineation and also across each of the three industrial typologies. While Porter considers that environmental changes, especially short-term ones, do not affect firms differently and are, therefore, not relevant for structural analysis or industry definition, the changes, especially in terms of emerging markets and technological openness, are so transformational that Porter's 1980 thesis would need to be revisited.

The earlier chapters have already provided a number of retakes to the existing theory. Chapter 1 has argued why and how the theory of five forces of competitive strategy has to be a sub-model within a macro model of five important economic forces. Chapter 2 proposed that in the alternative, firms should at least consider global liquidity as the most potent economic force and add it as the sixth competitive force. Chapter 3 advocated the need to be less paranoid about competition and more welcoming about collaboration; in fact, Chapter 3 takes a contrarian view on the Darwinian approach of competitive strategy. Chapters 4 and 5 specifically focus on supplier power and buyer power respectively, outlining the changes to conventional wisdom. The following discussion summarises how basic industry-level competitive forces are affected by the four types of industry changes discussed above.

Threat of entry

The first competitive force is the threat of new entrants to an industry. This threat is moderated by the barriers to entry present in an industry and countered by the reaction from existing competitors. According to Porter, there are six major sources of barriers to industry: economies of scale, product differentiation, capital requirements, switching costs, access to distribution channels and government policy. Major changes in industrial outsourcing to emerging markets over the past three decades have altered the impact of the first three sources, namely, scale, differentiation and capital. Design and manufacturing is no longer a 'first world' monopoly; it is a comparative advantage of rapidly emerging markets such as China and India. The wide development of the Internet has altered the dynamics of switching costs and distribution channels. Reformist government policies have facilitated rather than inhibited globalisation.

The only proprietary advantage that any firm can retain as an entry barrier in the changed environment, across all industries, is control over electronics and digitisation and the power of corporate and product brands. The ability to collaborate creatively aids reconfiguration in industries; in transformed industries, the sway over the Internet adds to control, while in reinvented industries 'machine biology' holds the key. Clearly, entry barriers based on the age-old manufacturing technology paradigm have given way to ones based on a new range of communication, networking, automation and intelligence technologies. In the past, the pioneer had experience on its side as an ethereal barrier; today, the pioneer needs to be highly innovative to create entry barriers. Received wisdom teaches us that experience leads to better learning and thus better throughput and costing. As industries are reshaped based on new technologies, including self-learning technologies, the pioneer has the advantage of forming the market first but also runs the risk of differentiators gaining from the subsequent perfection of the pioneer's technology. Differentiators have been able to develop new overlays for the pioneer's technology to reduce the first incumbent's advantage. Electronics, telecommunications and systems software have the feature of multiple generations of technology leading to multiple experience curves. Proprietary development of multiple generations of technology is currently the only sustainable entry barrier.

Intensity of rivalry

The second entry barrier relates to the intensity of rivalry among existing competitors. In the past, this was essentially in terms of price competition, which operated independent of specifications, with value being induced by virtue of lower price and price being a function of the lower margins that a firm was able to afford at the minimum. Today, price competition is more sophisticated; it is in terms of the range of products that a firm is able to operate at different specifications and price points with different levels of user experience. Porter's theory on intensity of rivalry holds that numerous or equally balanced competitors, slow industrial growth, high fixed or storage costs, lack of differentiation or switching costs, large capacity increments, diverse competitors, high strategic stakes and high exit barriers, either individually or in combinations, add to the intensity of rivalry in an industry.

Today, these parameters do not operate the way Porter envisaged them. The canvas for industry rivalry has shifted to emerging markets. Slow growth, induced partly by economic deceleration, has prompted firms in advanced countries to seek low-cost products and services from emerging markets, through collaborative arrangements, joint ventures or wholly owned subsidiaries. Renault's Kwid small car, developed in India, is an example. At the same time, the opening up and growth of emerging markets has prompted firms in advanced countries to seek a renewed and expanded presence in such markets for customer access. All this has led to intense rivalry among national and foreign firms for talent that can provide the competitive advantage. The focus has shifted from formulating competitive strategy to realising it through appropriate talent in emerging markets. The four new industrial typologies represent a new battleground for heightened rivalry in both advanced and emerging markets with interconnectivity of factor and customer inputs.

Pressure from substitute products

The third competitive force relates to pressure from substitute products. Porter rightly hypothesised that all firms in an industry compete, in a broad sense, with industries producing substitute products. As an example, Porter cites sugar and sugar substitutes. Identifying substitute products is a matter of searching for other products that can perform the same function as the industry's product. In Porter's 1980 analysis, the third competitive force of substitute products received rather perfunctory treatment compared to the first competitive force of entry or the second one of rivalry. In the contemporary world of technological convergence, however, the competitive force of substitute products is, in fact, the most intense. And, it works both ways in terms of unexpected substitutability as well as non-substitutability, challenging traditional structural analysis. With respect to the sugar example, the emerging trend is to move away from sugar substitutes and instead use other nutritious nuts and condiments that could provide near-sweet impact with additional nutritious value.

In the infrastructure space, hydro power, thermal power and nuclear power could be considered perfect substitutes. In the post-Fukushima tsunami world, nuclear energy has ceased to be a perfect substitute for other sources of power, at least in Japan and Germany. Renewable energy or solar energy development is being seen as a viable choice with improvements in technologies and adequate governmental incentives. The clean energy technologies could also decentralise generation and distribution of power to local communities, marking a fundamental change from the current models of power generation and distribution. The structural determinants for the competitive force of substitute products must, therefore, now include government policies. On the other hand, certain other segments of new generation industries offer the paradox of product convergence and usage divergence. The continuous emergence of laptops, notebooks, netbooks, smart phones, tablets and convertibles demonstrates how connectivity is functionalised in multiple ways even as all functionalities are integrated technologically. Product or service substitution needs to be a mega competitive force in any revised model of structural analysis.

Bargaining power of buyers

Bargaining power of buyers is the fourth competitive force. Buyers or customers are considered basic enablers for industry formation. Porter, however, takes a slightly contrarian view, stating that buyers compete with the industry by forcing down prices, bargaining for higher quality or more services and playing competitors against each other, all at the expense of industry profitability. This view is not only antithetical to the concept of the customer being the very purpose of a corporation but also uncharitable to the crucial roles consumerism and consumer activism play. The reality is that current buyers are eager to expend more of their valuable resources, time or money, to lap up an ever-increasing array of products and services being churned out by fiercely competing firms. Buyer groups or central purchasing organisations, especially those backed by large corporations, governments and large utilities such as electricity boards and hospitals, are no doubt more powerful than ever. Part of the enhanced power is due to technology, with e-auctions and e-bids setting the stage for enhanced and invisible competition.

Porter's model must consider that buyer power in today's world is scaled up by the firms themselves; an unending quest for market share and an unceasing wave of technological developments are now combining to prompt buyers to demand better features. Market expansion and market segmentation are now inescapable in any industry, to serve customers more perceptively rather than minimise the impact of buyer power. Firms need to recognise that as their products create new user segments, the balance of power is constantly shifted across buyer groups. Latest technologies create products and services that shift customers from existing products and services and also attract new or *naïve* customers to such products and services. Buyer power for such products and services enhances only when new generations of products and services are created. Clearly, buyer power is not a static competitive force in today's industrial scenario. Its dynamism is triggered by the rate of technological change, and by the multiple ways in which the boundaries of technology are redrawn.

Bargaining power of suppliers

Porter's model considers the bargaining power of suppliers as the fifth competitive force. Porter states that suppliers can exert bargaining power over participants in an industry by threatening to raise prices or reduce the quality of purchased goods and services. Porter's hypothesis on bargaining power of suppliers is rooted in classic industrial economics and does not recognise either the new platforms of supplier power or the collaborative nuances of contemporary supply-chain management. Newer platforms of commodity and metal exchanges have emerged as instruments that drive product prices up or down. Control over product prices no longer rests with suppliers, given the shared intent to benefit from market expansion that competitive products can help achieve. Both end-users and suppliers are now waking up to the advantages of strategic collaboration to ensure continued supply of low-cost, high-quality components and materials.

The new supply-chain model is insensitive to scale but sensitive to technology. That vendors of the day supply millions of components for new products does not mean that they can automatically dictate higher prices. Similarly, equipment makers are no longer viewing multi-sourcing as a means to reduce supplier power. Wise manufacturers now realise that their vendors need scale not merely to sustain themselves but more importantly to reduce costs and enhance quality. At the same time, the complex interrelationships of owned and licensed patents and cross-supply of designs and components or assemblies are muting supplier power in the face of advantages of joint development of industries and markets. The model of the Japanese auto makers working with their component and material manufacturers to optimise technologies is now more universal.

Bargaining Power of Suppliers	High	Low-Medium	High-Medium	Low
Bargaining Power of Buyers	High	Low-Medium	High-Medium	High
Pressure from Substitute Products	High	Low-Medium	High-Medium	Low
Intensity of Rivalry	High	Low-Medium	High-Medium	Low
Threat of Entry	High	Low-Medium	Medium	Low
Competitive Force ↑ → Industry Change	Reinforcement	Reconfiguration	Transformation	Reinvention
Digital Impact on Industry Change and Competitive Forces				

Figure 11.1
Structural Analysis

Figure 11.1 summarises the interrelationships between the five industry-level competitive forces and the four types of structural change in the industry. Reinforcement experiences the highest levels of competitive threats while re-invention rides over competitive forces rather easily. The other two types of structural changes, reconfiguration and transformation, are affected in different ways as demonstrated. In general, the higher the level of uniqueness a firm achieves through digitisation, the lower the threat of competitive forces.

Competitive strategy

Porter summarises his thesis on the structural analysis of industries by stating that once the forces affecting competition in an industry and their underlying causes have been diagnosed, the firm can formulate its competitive strategy. According to Porter, an effective competitive strategy takes offensive or defensive action to create a defendable position against the five competitive forces. Elaborating, Porter states that this would involve positioning the firm for the best defence, influencing the balance of forces through strategic moves or anticipating change and responding with an appropriate strategy. In summary, Porter proposes a relatively static structural analysis of the industry to lead to a dynamic strategy formulation by the firm.

As this chapter demonstrates, the issue with Porter's framework in the contemporary world is that industries are being reshaped by new technological trends at a far greater pace than in the past, and the sources of organic (or in-house) competitive advantage are far fewer than those obtained in the past. While the five competitive forces remain valid as a core concept, their structural determinants have changed significantly over the past three decades. More dynamic and more expanded models of structural analysis are needed. These must be customised to reinforced, reconfigured, transformed and reinvented industries as identified here, with a more flexible definition of industry and a more perceptive identification of competitive forces and sources of competitive advantage, developed essentially on technological dimensions.

Chapter 12
Cost Leadership and Quality Leadership

Total Quality, Cost and Time Management (TQCTM): A Relevant Competitive Paradigm for India Inc.

- Cost leadership is not low-cost production; it includes leadership in quality and safety for given functionalities.
- The belief that a firm should continuously work on a best-in-class quality-cost position is the fundamental tenet that differentiates an industry leader from the rest.
- Total Cost Management (TCM) and Total Quality Management (TQM) are two independent, though quite interrelated, streams of a firm that are integrated by technology.
- Cost and quality integration require a managerial mindset that utilises technology and human resources in perfect harmony.

Cost is the ultimate indicator of a firm's competitiveness. Porter, therefore, accords significant importance to cost leadership as a generic competitive strategy. This ties in well with the industrial economics approach that resonates throughout Porter's work in terms of scale and scope building, share increases, economics of integration and so on. That said, Porter's work does not fully discuss the semantics and optics of cost leadership. In line with Porter's proposal, cost leadership must emerge from productivity and efficiency all along the value chain. It presupposes maintenance of quality.

In reality though, global instances highlight the pitfalls of pursuing cost leadership without a comprehensive appreciation of the cost paradigm. Cost leadership is not the same as low-cost production. Neither is it related to arbitrary elimination of processes and qualifications. It is not even reengineering a product on a 'fit for purpose' mission. While cost leadership has much to do with frugal engineering and lean operations, it cannot be allowed to lose sight of leadership in quality and safety for given functionalities. This chapter discusses the importance of cost leadership from a total enterprise perspective and in the process, presents a significantly upgraded concept of cost leadership as relevant for competitive strategy.

Cost, quality and competitiveness

Cost management is the most important instrument in India Inc.'s quest for globalisation. Cost, however, should never be seen independent of Quality. In all ways, cost and quality are significantly interrelated. There are several myths surrounding the cost-quality equation. The most prominent one is that cost and quality are adversely correlated. In other words, it is assumed that higher quality leads to higher cost and somewhat conversely lower cost implies lower quality. While higher levels of quality do require higher levels of product specification, material strength, manufacturing integrity and service delivery, the relationship is neither linear nor proportionate. A higher quality product or service actually creates and expands demand, enables higher scale of production and distribution, improves overhead absorption and ultimately results in a superior cost position. Quality-integrated cost management is an essential tool for competitiveness.

The ability to successfully operate on low margins is the ultimate test of a firm's cost-competitiveness. Often, firms, especially those operating in the innovation and niche space, believe that cost is secondary and differentiation is primary. Some firms may even believe that the pursuit of cost leadership and product differentiation are contrarian. There is, in fact, no conflict in the pursuit of these twin goals. Elimination and avoidance of all non-value adding and wasteful activities and infusion and integration of value-adding activities is a primary strategy of all corporations that have accomplished sustainable profitable growth. A review of all corporations that have had such growth over the past several decades in multiple industries and multiple regions, from Toyota in Japan to IBM in USA, reflects this basic philosophy.

Controllable factors

Often, firms have a rather simplistic view of costs and competition. Many leaders are apt to exhort their employees to control what is under their control—namely costs, capacity and production—and not worry too much about factors not under their control, for example, prices, demand and competition. Nothing can be farther from the truth than this. In fact, all factors mentioned above, whether apparently controllable or not, fall squarely within the responsibility and control of firms. Low market demand is often an indicator of the unacceptable quality-cost position of a product or service. Another player's lower-priced, equivalent or superior quality product or service in the market is an indicator of the superior cost-quality position such a player has been able to achieve relative to the incumbent. Competition in an industry through new offerings indicates that the industry is attractive in terms of growth and profitability parameters.

In essence, a firm cannot believe that its costs alone are a concern and not how a competitor prices its products. The belief that a firm should continuously work on a best-in-class quality-cost position is the fundamental tenet that differentiates an industry leader from the rest. This is not to suggest that all firms in an industry must aspire for such an industry-leading position. A firm's strategy is the result not merely of its leadership aspirations but also of its technical and managerial capabilities, capital and other resource endowments and the legacy issues relating to historical evolution. The point is that a firm should anchor its growth and sustainability strategies on a comprehensive strategy of quality-integrated cost management. To do so, firms must recognise that quality and cost are supported by individually unique clusters of factors that determine the levels of each and their interrelationship that a firm can enjoy.

Cost-quality levers

Cost is a powerful indicator of the competitiveness of a firm in an industry in which all constituent firms can provide products or services of comparable quality. The levers that a firm possesses to establish a position of superior cost are: productivity (or efficiency and effectiveness combined), scale, scope and speed. Encompassing all this is a zero-waste approach. Each of these factors is interrelated and their harmonious integration requires detailed planning and correct execution with high forecast and delivery accuracy. Here, forecast accuracy is a broad concept covering not merely forecasting of demand but also of resources such as people, finance, materials, equipment and other inputs required for operations and delivery. Total cost management, therefore, requires the application of appropriate levers, as identified here, across the entire value chain.

Quality is a powerful indicator of the ultimate competitiveness of a firm in an industry in which all constituent firms can provide products and services of comparable cost. The levers that a firm possesses to establish a position of superior quality are: innovation, product and service specifications, process specifications (covering both technical and non-technical processes), safety, skill levels of employees and compliance systems. Encompassing all this is a zero-defect approach. Each of these factors is interrelated and a superior position on quality can emerge only based on integration of all these parameters across the value chain, with a 'first time right' approach. Concurrent engineering is a methodology that has been successfully deployed by the automobile industry, especially the Japanese automobile industry, to ensure quality in a seamless and unfailing manner across the total value chain. Compliance to stringent benchmarks is important for ensuring high quality, and the challenge for organisations is in simultaneously conforming as well as innovating to meet such benchmarks. Total quality management, therefore, requires application of the appropriate quality levers, as identified here, across the entire value chain. Figure 12.1 depicts the cost-quality cluster levers.

Figure 12.1
Cost-Quality Cluster Levers

Technology and management as integrators

The foregoing discussion may lead one to consider Total Cost Management (TCM) and Total Quality Management (TQM) as two independent, but rather interrelated, streams of a firm. The point that each influences the other positively is well-taken by firms but they grapple with the challenge of achieving such integration. The key to such integration lies in technology, be it product, service, manufacturing, distribution or information technology. Product and process technologies present themselves in terms of the right form factor, appropriate levels of consumption of appropriate types of materials, the conversion efficiencies in terms of uptime, cycle time, yields and so on.

Service and distribution technologies present options for the firms and consumers to interconnect supplies and requirements in a seamless function. Information technology (IT) helps the total value chain to be efficient and effective and to eliminate waste and ensure compliance to specifications.

Equally important is the management of a firm, which comprises a host of factors from organisational culture to individual competencies. TCM and TQM aspirations cannot be fulfilled merely by deploying technologies. Just as every activity in a firm is fundamentally behaviour driven, cost and quality require a managerial mindset that utilises technology and human resources in perfect harmony. The overall industrial context, including its strategic evolution, and the nature of competitive forces determine how management should deploy technology and human resources. What industries considered a luxury in research and workshop settings a few decades ago, namely automation, has now become commonplace with the advances in mechatronics (electronics-integrated mechanical engineering) and has vastly changed expectations on what constitutes good ergonomics and wise economics. At the same time, an employee's fundamental capabilities continue to determine how a national or global value chain comprising several functions, sites, teams and technologies can be seamlessly integrated.

Time as the ultimate arbiter

With several firms competing for similar strategic space, and all of them pursuing superior quality-cost options, it becomes necessary to identify one additional calibrator for superior positioning. In this context, time—the most precious, non-renewable and non-regenerative resource—becomes critically important. Here again, myths surround the concepts of quality-cost execution in a timeframe. It is not true, for example, that faster work could carry the risk of lower quality or that greater time allocation would *ipso facto* provide greater quality. Often, hidden or implicit activities need to be performed and not performing these could have adverse quality and cost implications. Curing of concrete in a construction activity is one such example. There could also be limitations in the extent of parallel processing that can be carried out in a multi-task project. Components of a new design watch, for example, cannot be ordered unless the basic design parameters, both product and manufacturing, are frozen.

Cost leadership, as discussed in other chapters of this book too, is important for all types of firms. At the very least, it helps firms to battle commoditisation and at the very best, it helps even innovators enjoy great margins. The foregoing discussion has brought out many facets of cost leadership that go beyond financial numbers; it is an integrated management paradigm. The very special attribute of rendering the highest quality work at the lowest cost possible and in the shortest timeframe possible differentiates a firm from others who take only pure cost positions or even combined cost and quality positions. Samsung's huge recall costing billions of dollars with its prestigious Note 7 smart device is yet another indicator of the need for a fine balance between cost, quality and time, failing which firms could face debilitating adversities. The Total Quality, Cost and Time Management (TQCTM) paradigm is an integrated and holistic strategic platform of competitive strategy that is highly relevant for an India Inc., which is seeking an ever-expanding presence in the globalised economic and industrial world.

Chapter 13
Differentiation and De-Commoditisation

Differentiation versus De-commoditisation: Strategies for Haves and Have-nots

- Differentiation ranks next to innovation as a value-building, remunerative strategy in product and business development.
- Commoditisation is a direct consequence of lack of technological development on the one hand and excess competition on the other.
- Firms that have typical technological and market competencies are truly firms of destiny for differentiation.
- De-commoditisation can be effected in three ways: value adding features in a commoditised product, modifying a product to deliver additional principal functions and retro-designing a product to rediscover its roots.

Porter's second generic strategy relates to differentiation. Differentiation requires a product or service to have certain unique attributes that the competitor's products or services do not have. Typically, differentiation involves a fair degree of innovation related to such attributes and requires some efforts even by pioneers to replicate them. Unlike cost leadership which is heavily internal focused, differentiation is external focused in terms of identifying what provides uniqueness in the market place. The earlier chapters have touched upon what Porter suggests are the compulsions and enablers for differentiation from the perspective of competitive strategy. Contemporary developments have, however, queered the pitch for meaningful differentiation. A concomitant of rapid technological progress is the rapid commoditisation of technologies. It has become easier for even follower firms to attempt minor differentiation based on widely available technologies. Unlike Porter's formulation of differentiation as a selective strategy, it has become a strategy that is more replicable than ever. This chapter discusses de-commoditisation as a seemingly contrarian concept that is actually a companion strategy to differentiation.

Understanding differentiation

Differentiation ranks next to innovation as a value-building, remunerative strategy in product and business development. As a strategy, it evolves along with industry structure. When an industry is built around a first-time pioneering monopoly product, differentiation is of academic interest as the product constitutes the entire industry. As new players with identical or similar products enter the industry, differentiation emerges as the factor that sets firms apart. However, when competition reaches a saturation point, the feasibility of differentiation declines while the importance of cost leadership climbs. Popularly, when competition becomes intense and differentiation becomes difficult a product is seen as a commodity product. As an axiom, differentiation tends to be inversely correlated with commoditisation and *vice versa*. Yet, firms with investible resources could pursue differentiation as a premium strategy even in commoditised industries.

Differentiation tends to be primarily on product technology. In certain cases, it can be in terms of branding, channel marketing and point-of-sale strategies. Technology-driven differentiation tends to be more robust and sustainable than other forms of differentiation. Firms can seek to be differentiated not only by offering highly unique products but also by offering a diverse range of products. In many cases, single-product differentiation becomes vulnerable and firms are forced to field a broad range of products to meet multiple consumer needs. At one point, Maruti-Suzuki held almost 100 percent of the Indian car market with only one product, the 800cc car. Yet, its dependence on small cars coupled with the entry of other global car manufacturers in India caused Maruti-Suzuki to cede 50 percent of its share to competition. Diversity for a firm leads to differentiation of sorts; it does not, however, stop commoditisation. Many analysts equate commoditisation with products becoming generic copycats and *vice versa*. This, however, is not necessarily true.

Commodity

In strategic discourse, commoditisation is a concept that is used rather extensively as a driver or outcome of competition. Alongside innovation and differentiation, commoditisation figures more prominently as an inevitable concomitant of a rapidly developing industry structure. Commoditisation is a direct consequence of the lack of technological development on the one hand, easy availability of platform technologies, and excess competition on the other. It is now hypothesised that no industry, however technologically advanced, can escape commoditisation. For example, unbridled competition in smart phones is making high-technology products look like commodity products, freely available off-shelf—proof that no product group can escape the spectre of commoditisation. However, commoditisation is not just related to competition. Understanding the theorem of commoditisation in strategic parlance requires an understanding of the word itself. Common words often get layered with folklore, especially in strategic discourse!

Simply put, commodity is a raw material or product that can be bought and sold. Some analysts believe that materials that do not have differentiating characteristics are free commodities. Others believe that even when no differentiation exists, the demand-supply equation determines if certain products are precious commodities. Some commodities like oil, gold and water, which are, in varying degrees, non-renewable natural resources, tend to be precious. Some commodities like grains and metals whose production can be stimulated tend to be more freely available. Some believe that products and materials that are nature's gift are commodities, while products and materials that are worked by human design and manufacture are non-commodities. Even this approach does not work because a product of great human effort like steel is often considered a commodity. In a sense, there is no straight correlation, in any combination, between natural occurrence, human development, preciousness and differentiation that can define commoditisation.

Commoditised shakeout

Commoditisation is the result of numerous factors: abundant natural availability, ready usability, shared characteristics, surfeit of capacity, basic need fulfilment and so on. Any product, even one reflecting the highest level of human ingenuity, can become commoditised with time. Any commodity could also turn precious and differentiated if it ceases to be naturally available, like gold. A commodity could become differentiated if it can be worked on to imbue special characteristics, for example, diamonds that are cut uniquely. If a commodity like oil can be developed to reduce friction and pollutants, it becomes differentiated. When first introduced, a mutual-fund instrument could have been very special, but today it is completely undifferentiated and commoditised. The same would be true of a special lending instrument like housing finance; it was differentiated by a specially established institution, Housing Development Finance Corporation, but with all banks treating housing finance as a key component of their lending portfolio, the instrument has become commoditised.

Commoditisation is a concomitant of two principal factors: easy availability of materials and easy availability of technologies. Together, they determine the height of entry barriers to an industry. The first response of firms and industries to this phenomenon is to drive down entry barriers even more, almost to the level of an industry shakeout. Emerging markets such as India are particularly prone to commoditised shakeouts. Several industries, as diverse as motor pumps, lubricating oils, airlines, television channels, home foods and bulk drugs, to name a few, have witnessed commoditised shakeout. The strategy adopted by most firms, when faced with commoditisation, is to seek cost leadership to avoid being the victims of a shakeout. This strategy has a floor-level cost price, below which it cannot be pursued, except at the risk of self-annihilation. The ideal strategy to address this is to have differentiated products across the firms but it is easier said than done. As mentioned earlier, only a few firms that possess high technology and resources can hope to pursue differentiation in the face of commoditisation; these are the 'Haves.' If differentiation is for the Haves, the 'Have-nots' need a relevant strategy as proposed herein. In fact, de-commoditisation is the other side of the coin for differentiation! Figure 13.1 represents the differentiation-commoditisation matrix.

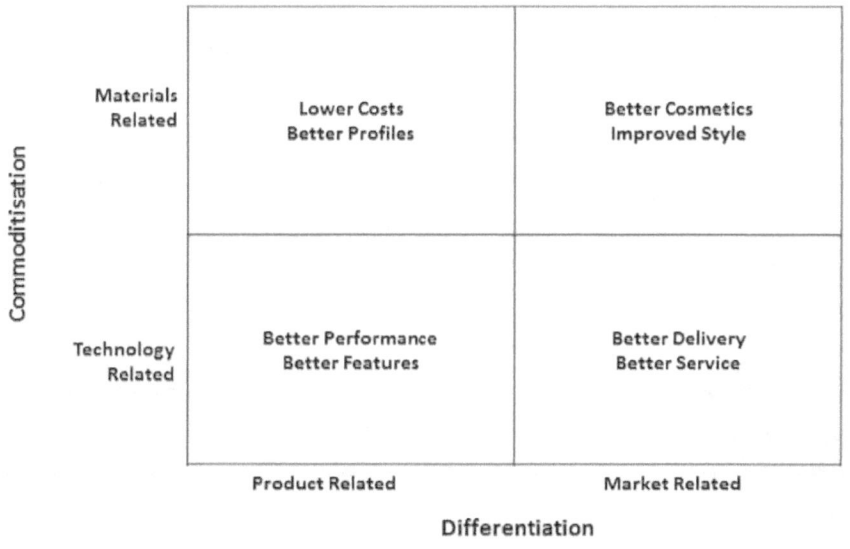

Figure 13.1
Differentiation-Commoditisation Matrix

Differentiation for the Haves

Differentiation is not merely a function of financial resources. It requires visionary ideation and smart strategising. Technology that continually fulfils higher levels of needs helps in differentiation. Basic human needs of communication and socialisation are continuously expressed through different levels of technology, from early telegraphy to modern satellite communication, and from classic landline phones to voice-over-internet protocols. Socialisation has kept pace with communication technologies but has essentially utilised communication portals and cloud infrastructure. Future technologies could be extensions of human intellectual and physical activities. Socialisation can take the reverse route to induct robots as part of everyday life. These kinds of differentiation require two types of Haves, those with technological innovation as the first core competency and customer outreach as the second.

The possession of these core competencies enables firms to continuously innovate new products that fulfil human needs in completely different manners. Those who utilise the core competencies to undertake only incremental innovations cannot achieve true differentiation; on the other hand, they deliver small incremental improvements through high levels of technology, leading to adverse cost-value relationships. Firms that have typical technological and market competencies are truly firms of destiny for differentiation. While the pioneers qualify almost naturally for the differentiator role (for example, Cadbury's in milk chocolates, Danone in dairy products, Kellogg's in breakfast cereals), new differentiators emerge (for example, Nestle with KitKat). The Haves should rightfully concentrate on utilising their core competencies to set newer product trajectories. Given that differentiation requires significant investments (though not on the same scale as innovation), the Have-nots would need a different approach.

De-commoditisation for the Have-nots

On one level, de-commoditisation is responsible business management. It avoids trivialisation of a product through self-destructing strategies. The launch of a new product at a huge price premium that is immediately followed by buybacks and cash-back discounts trivialises technologies and products. The first step towards commoditisation is an almost unintended consequence of volume-driven marketing or cost reduction. The right de-commoditisation strategy is to hold, and if possible even reinforce, product specifications through the introduction and growth phases of a product life cycle, even in the face of new competition (through differentiation or cost leadership). The second step in de-commoditisation is to avoid frivolous market segmentation. While offering products at different value points is inescapable, mindless jumbling up of specifications to drive up product proliferation adds to commoditisation. The right de-commoditisation strategy is to keep the product line-up simple and meaningful.

The next challenge of de-commoditisation arises when the inevitability of commoditisation happens. De-commoditisation can happen in one of three ways. The first is by building value adding features in a commoditised product (for example, extending a yogurt product in two directions of low-fat range and high-energy range). The second is modifying a product to deliver two principal functions in place of one (for example, making a gaming device like Kinetic that helps gaming as well as exercising). The third is retro-designing a product to rediscover its roots (for example, bringing smart watch technologies to conventional Swiss watches). De-commoditisation requires a disciplined Kaizen mindset that always upholds a product's value in the eyes and heart of the consumer. It will not require the mega investments that the Haves splurge on differentiation drivers but will certainly need a keen eye for detail and a penchant for simplicity and functionality in a mindset of quality. Figure 13.2 represents the three-step process of de-commoditisation.

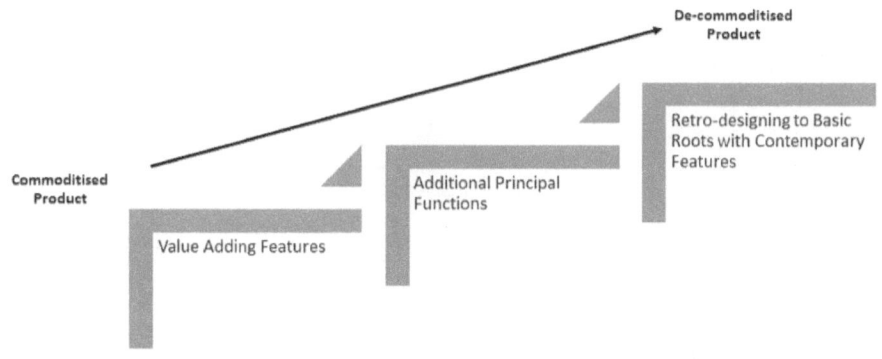

Figure 13.2
Three Steps of De-commoditisation

De-commoditisation is, in a sense, a more universally beneficial strategy which both Haves and Have-nots can adopt. However, it clearly makes more strategic sense for the Haves to pursue innovation or differentiation and for the Have-nots to pursue de-commoditisation.

Chapter 14
Niche as a Core Competence

Niche as a Sustainable Competitive Strategy

- Niche strategy focuses on a narrow market segment with competitive superiority through cost leadership or differentiation; it requires abilities that others in the industry do not have.
- Niche products and markets are rarely static; they vanish and redevelop over time. They are created by innovation in terms of product technologies or marketing processes.
- Skillsets and competencies required for a niche strategy, in turn, require a broad operational base in an industry.
- Niche does not define industry; nor does industry determine niche. It is neither a product strategy nor a marketing one. It is, in essence, more a competency than a strategy.

As discussed earlier, Porter proposes three generic competitive strategies which any firm can pursue, subject to certain covenants. These are cost leadership, differentiation and niche. Earlier chapters have presented how the classic formats of cost leadership and differentiation need redefinition to address contemporary challenges. Cost leadership cannot exist without quality leadership and time effectiveness, while differentiation has to guard against de-commoditisation. Porter's third generic strategy, focus or niche, is a popular and fashionable term in strategic parlance. Many corporate leaders prefer their firms to be niche players rather than mass players, to articulate their premium positioning. There is, however, an inadequate appreciation of what constitutes niche and where niche fits in a firm's quest for scale and scope as much as for revenue and profitability. This chapter clears some popular misconceptions and establishes some logical foundations for niche strategy.

Niche as a concept

The focus strategy concentrates on a narrow market segment and within that, achieves competitive superiority through either cost leadership or differentiation.

There are many interpretations of niche as a strategy. The physical definition of niche is that of a crevice where one can be safely ensconced. The managerial definition of niche is one of a unique product-market segmentation by which a firm can enjoy low competition and high profits. Although a product or service is often seen to lead to a niche position, it is market segmentation that enables premium pricing and dictates the need for niche products and services. Niche as a concept is not new. From Ferrari, Rolls Royce and Jaguar in the automobile industry to Omega, Rolex and Tudor in the watch industry, niche strategy is as old as the beginning of industrialisation and as new as the challenge of competitiveness.

Earlier, the concept of niche was based on developing and manufacturing products with a high level of sophistication and, therefore, with a high cost and a price premium that only certain segments of the markets could accept. Niche was associated with the pride of ownership of a premium brand. Niche strategy thus involved a significant marketing and promotional input. Niche also came to be interpreted in terms of a differentiated product catering to a very specific and narrow segment. In modern times, however, niche strategy needs to be a much more inclusive concept. It is no longer about identifying a slot that others would not (or cannot) address but rather about retaining invincibility and sustainability despite ingress of intense competition. Today, niche is the possession of an ability or set of abilities that most firms in the industry do not have. Apple demonstrates what niche, as relevant to the contemporary times, can do for corporate strategy and performance, with premium positioning while also serving the broader market.

Apple 'i Products'

Apple Inc., led by Steve Jobs, virtually rewrote the book of strategy and the history of consumer electronics, with its pioneering 'i Products': the iPod, iPhone and iPad. These products are differentiated with features that multiple niche market segments would appreciate and pay for but are also value-competitive as a total package, helping most people become users. The niches that each of the products occupy, therefore, cover almost the entire market place questioning the very definition of niche. The introduction of iPod, iPhone and iPad generated numerous competitors, yet these products remain the pioneers with an amazing standing. The sustainability of Apple products relates to the fact that they ushered in and successfully maintained a whole new and complete user experience that could not be matched by competitor products in totality despite being superior in parts. They were highly effective products with a distinctive Apple ecosystem that were offered to customers with attractive ownership options and distinctive retailing formats. However, the products constituted the core that created the markets.

Apple iPod provided for the user, for the first time, a total digital audio-visual experience in the most miniaturised and most elegant form factor, with memory levels unprecedented at the time of introduction in January 2001. Eventually, iPod emerged as a well-segmented product family of Shuffle, Nano, Classic and Touch, meeting different user needs. The iPod user experience was heightened by the Net-based proprietary iTunes which provided thousands of tunes to music lovers owning the iPods. Apple iPhone, introduced in January 2007, provided, for the first time, a total convergence experience for the smart phone user, again with the most elegant and user friendly form factor and vastly superior memory levels with hundreds of applications in its iTunes store. Apple iPad, released in April 2010, took the niche revolution forward, focusing on media and gaming applications with ease of portability for home or office and static or dynamic use. Apple iPod, iPhone and iPad thus represented a unique fusion of state-of-the-art design and manufacturing on the one hand and cutting-edge hardware and software on the other. All the three product streams received continuous enhancements; iPod with touch and enhanced media technology and iPhone with all-round enhancements over seven generations, and iPad with professional work and superior media capability.

Shifting sand dunes

Niche products and markets are rarely static. They move, vanish and redevelop over time. In India's trucking industry of the 1980s, Heavy Duty Vehicles (HDVs), manufactured almost exclusively by Ashok Leyland, constituted a niche product group and a niche market for the company. With the enhancements in freight haulage patterns and improvements in highway network as well as the entry of new players such as Volvo, Benz, MAN, and Navistar (besides the incumbent Tata Motors) into the heavy haulage segment, HDVs no longer constitute a niche. In the 1990s, a shopping mall would have been a niche retailing format or a multiplex would have been a niche cinematic experience in India. Today, shopping malls and multiplexes are commonplace with high competition. Dual-time, multiple time zone or analogue-digital watches could have been niche watch technologies a few years ago. These are now offered virtually by all watch makers. A decade ago, touch technology in cellular phones was a practical impossibility; within five years it dominated cellular phones and further extended to notebooks and netbooks. At the time of its launch, 3D viewing technology was highly niche, whether for cinema or television, but 3D movies and 3D televisions are commonplace today. Such examples are indeed numerous.

Niche products and markets are verily created by innovation in product technologies or marketing processes. However, as follow-on products, analogue products and even enhanced products are developed and marketing becomes more intense with additional competitors, a niche strategy of the present could be challenged by the time of actual commercialisation or a few years after commercialisation. It is, therefore, necessary that firms that aim to follow niche strategy are always at the top of the curve, constantly defining new user experiences, seeking enhancements in current niche products or exploring avenues for a new generation of niche products. Even a series of successive niche products would at some point of time face saturation dictating the need for a breakthrough move to a new niche trajectory. The emerging era of a 2-in-1 convertible providing the flexibility of tablet and laptop computers is a contemporary example of the trajectory of a niche strategy moving higher.

When narrow needs breadth

Developing the skillsets and competencies required for a niche strategy requires a broad operational base in an industry. A niche strategy, which by definition tends to be exclusive to premium market segments, may provide robust profitability but not necessarily huge revenues. The Swiss watch industry, especially the hand-crafted watch segment, was an example of a niche-driven industrial operation; the niche was in terms of elegance, precision and quality. However, in terms of scale and scope, the Swiss watch industry became a marginal player in the 1980s and 1990s relative to the nimbler, more efficient and more diversified Japanese watchmakers. Only after it integrated new research and manufacturing technologies with its traditional niche of elegance and precision did the Swiss industry become a global force again.

Firms and leadership teams that pursue a niche strategy cannot build business and operational models only on niche. An ability to develop and manufacture a broad range of products, in fact, helps the firm to support niche technology not only financially but also organisationally, with a scale that can attract the highly talented professionals who can deliver a niche platform. In several circumstances, niche emerges as a high level capability of a pyramid of normal, organisational competency hierarchy. The ability of Toyota to develop clean hybrid cars (for example, Prius) is a result of its ability to have a large and broad spectrum car manufacturing capability. On the other hand, a pure electric car manufacturer is unlikely to have either the scale or scope sufficient to support a sole, narrow niche strategy. Even a leading fragrance manufacturer such as Elizabeth Arden positions designer and premium fragrances on a base of hundreds of finely segmented cosmetics and perfumes.

Value chain fragments

Niche does not define industry; nor does industry determine niche. Yet many strategists fail to view niche and industry in proper perspectives. A full-fledged integrated pharmaceutical player may view an independent, drug-discovery entity as a niche operation. This view is based wholly on the very special capabilities required to invent and develop new pharmaceutical products. On the other hand, a broad-based drug-discovery entity may consider a similar discovery entity specialising in just one therapeutic area as a niche player. Conceptually, each segment or sub-segment of an industrial value chain may appear to be a potential niche segment. Analytically, however, a strategy based on value-chain fragmentation would qualify more as an optic of industry definition while one based on competitiveness of specialisation would be more reflective of a true niche. Figure 14.1 summarises what niche is and what it is not.

Niche…	
is dependent on industry	✗
defines industry	✗
is product strategy	✗
is marketing strategy	✗
is an organisational competency	✓

Figure 14.1
Niche Dashboard

By corollary, moving up the value chain of a product group does not necessarily confer a niche position. A manufacturer of value-added steel products need not necessarily be a more successful niche player than a steel producer who has mastered the customisation of basic steel specifications to a wide variety of applications. If at all, the broad-based yet customised basic steel producer could have a better position as a successful niche player. To cite another example, while industrial biotechnology (classic fermentation) is commoditised, evolution of biotechnology in terms of mammalian cell culture and later plant and other DNA-based developments led to a reinvention of the basic biotechnology value chain. To be a niche player, therefore, one has to look beyond industry or value-chain definitions and focus more on the fundamentals of science, technology and management that make a product or service truly unassailable.

Niche as a competency

Niche is neither a product strategy nor a marketing strategy. It is, in essence, more a competency than strategy. BlackBerry has as its core competence high-security encrypted communication; if it brings this to play in a general Android phone, it makes the phone a niche product. This and the other examples cited in this chapter demonstrate that a sustainable niche strategy requires a series of successive innovative products that are proactively and competitively produced and differentiated in the marketplace in terms of their user experience. At some point, even successive product enhancements would need to leapfrog into a totally new configuration. For example, after a series of successive improvements in iPod, iPhone and iPad, the next wave could be in terms of a multi-purpose hand-held artificial intelligence device for a totally new technological and user experience. This sort of evolution and transformation in niche positioning requires complete end-to-end capability in terms of fundamental innovation, nimble product development, lean manufacturing and aggressive marketing.

Implied in a niche strategy are several other attributes, such as the ability to organically develop or globally source the best technologies and components, to project-manage the processes of concurrent engineering and targeted product launch and to network with various collaborating partners. Ability to innovate and differentiate on a product-market dimension with low-cost global supply-chain capabilities, high-end manufacturing efficiencies and broad-spectrum marketing capabilities requires a set of organisational competencies that are industry leading in each domain. A niche strategy should be enduring based on competencies that can deliver sustainable value. A niche strategy thus needs to be seen as comprehensive, encompassing and integrating all three generic strategies proposed by Porter. An industry would have players following one of the three generic strategies proposed by Porter, but the real niche players would be the few who consciously develop the competencies required for a niche strategy.

Industry leadership

What constitutes true industry leadership is a question that can have several answers. At a simplistic level, scale is a major reckoner of leadership. However, as demonstrated by the virtual bankruptcy and the governmental bail-out of General Motors, once a global leader in automobiles, scale without profitability and sustainability has little meaning. Neither is a classic niche product positioning relevant in today's scenario as demonstrated by the compulsions on niche players to demonstrate really unique capabilities, failing which they face sale of brands or businesses to full-line companies. Even a niche player like Bose has a very large line-up of products. Industry leadership comes with broad-spectrum positioning that caters to a full market with as many products and as much cost efficiency as possible, while creating unique niches based on innovation in each product-market segment. The objective of industry leadership for a firm is thus predicated upon combining scale, scope and niche into one business model.

Some firms are in a position to drive up, in a largely monopolistic manner, all the parameters of product performance (and hence the user experience) by themselves. Intel is a good example of monopolistic product positioning; it has been able to dominate the industry with its successive generations of processors (despite the slippage in mobile chips). Similarly, Microsoft is able to dominate the software industry with its successive releases of operating systems. These are, however, exceptions rather than the rule and even such firms seek to expand their footprint as expansively as possible (an example is Intel manufacturing processors for all digital applications and Microsoft extending its Windows operating system from computers to mobile phones and tablets as well as convertibles, regardless of price points and manufacturers). Today, most firms, from Sony to Samsung, ABB to Siemens, and Toyota to Renault are under pressure to maximise product-market coverage while seeking appropriate niches. These firms have, however, developed their own sets of unique competencies to enable their own unique models of expansive niche strategies (for example, the well-known Toyota Production System and not so well-known but equally effective Toyota Development System, also called Set-Based Concurrent Engineering at Toyota).

Summary

The prescription for a firm seeking sustainable industry leadership would be combining product or service variety with innovation and excelling over other competitors by providing unique user experiences in each case. Cost competitiveness and differentiation must be fused into an integrated sustainable niche strategy, the conceptualisation and execution of which calls for a very special competence on the part of a firm. An extremely inventive, creative and integrated research-manufacturing-marketing paradigm that is enhanced by industry-leading capabilities in all supportive functions is the essence of niche as a firm-level competence.

Chapter 15
Strategic Comparators and Responders

Strategic Comparators and Responders: Reinventing Strategy Formulation

- Economic volatility and competitive dynamics require a more pervasive and expansive approach to strategy formulation.
- The wise firm must institutionalise strategic comparison and responsiveness as a strategic planning process ethic.
- Strategic comparators emerge as both metrics and scenarios. Strategic responders reset the firm's strategy in response to strategic comparators.
- Holistic strategic planning is an alchemy of techno-economic forecasting, competitive intelligence and organisational core competencies.

The most relevant but also most ignored fact of corporate strategy is that competitive strategy can rarely be drawn up in isolation. In any industry, the strategies pursued by individual firms affect not only the industry's structure but also the competitive strategies of all other constituent firms. Yet, firms and strategy leaders find it expedient to draw up strategies as though only they exist in the industry. It is not uncommon, for example, to see almost all firms in an industry aspiring to achieve growth rates above the industry average, move up the industry pecking order by a few notches, introduce industry-leading products, achieve the largest market share or secure the highest profitability. It is, therefore, not surprising that most achieve only patchy successes with their strategies and aspirations and only a few firms succeed in achieving their aspirations comprehensively.

Given that corporate strategy in a firm is typically drawn up at the level of the chief executive officer, chief strategy officer, chief financial officer and other CXOs, all with requisite capabilities, the introverted manner in which corporate strategy is drawn up defies logic. The reasons are often three pronged: structural, systemic and behavioural. Strategy is a highly complex intellectual activity that integrates established data as much as it factors in uncertain aspirations. The larger the organisation, the greater the need for inclusivity, calling for ground-level strategy development in all functions, domains and regions, with a sharp eye for internal and external factors. Yet, typically the strategy department is usually the smallest in a firm and also relatively cocooned from mainstream activities, thus limited by the ability to capture all the required nuances and details and conduct necessary sophisticated analyses.

Systemically, industrial managers and leaders, despite the strong managerial learning that emphasises coping with uncertainty with a wide range of tools, do not excel in deploying the right tools for various contexts. They tend to play upon the quantitative-qualitative divide based on the expediency of moving forward or stalling a decision. Behaviourally, professionals involved in strategy development tend to believe that strategy formulation is an esoteric science that can be carried out only by specialists. This factor and the distance strategists tend to create between themselves and other members of the organisation results in a disconnect between ground realities, capabilities of the broader organisation, aspirations of senior leaders and the potentialities of the organisation. These factors, and the lack of quality external data or the cost and time required to access such data, act as systemic deterrents to developing a comprehensive strategic canvas and achieving organisational inclusivity in strategy formulation.

Pitfalls of introverted strategy

Every strategist maintains that his or her strategic plan is developed based on opportunities and risks inherent in the economic environment and the likely moves of competitors. Apart from the fact that such claims are often no more than armchair predictions, the benefits of any strategic plan disappear the moment its first year is converted into the firm's monthly budget. This is because thereafter, the firm keeps monitoring its performance against the budget rather than external developments or competitor achievements. As a result, the firm misses out on the opportunity to overcome new challenges or spot new opportunities. As the economic environment becomes more volatile and competitive dynamics become more intense by the day, all professionals who treat strategy as an exclusive preserve must look at a more pervasive and expansive approach to strategy formulation.

A classic instance of the introverted strategy is found in certain recent developments in the top crust of the Indian IT industry. A top IT player was preoccupied with implementing strategies developed at the beginning of the economic downturn and was oblivious to the moves being made by other top players to build capacities as the global economy began to emerge from the woods. As a result, the firm lost its edge in consulting capacity and customer access and was relegated to a lower spot. Another IT player was so convinced of its own brand charisma that it did away with employee stock options for certain sections of employees only to discover later that attrition had shot up. An inability to assess or accept the superiority of other more effective mobile operating systems and a belief in its own proprietary system made a leading global mobile maker like Nokia lose the edge in smart phones. Several Indian pharmaceutical majors who have ignored the plans of late starters to aggressively establish capacities or create marketing organisations have seen their market share drop precipitously.

Directional stability for business and performance comparison vis-à-vis plans are extremely important for firms to stay focused. Given that most strategic investments such as capacity creation require lead times of several years and that even tactical operations such as inventory management involve lead times of months, it is impractical to have continuously dynamic plans, even if they are responsive to external developments. That said, given the fundamental responsibility of strategy formulators to deliver sustainable growth for the firm, innovative ways must be found to ensure internal stability while handling external volatility. While a firm may find that it is relatively easy to make internally focused plans based on internal factors and difficult to make externally focused plans requiring reliable external information, this should be the least of the reasons to stay only inward focused and in the process be oblivious of external developments. The wise firm must institutionalise strategic comparison and responsiveness as a strategic management ethic.

Key external themes

The theory of strategic comparators and responders proposed here is quite different from the existing concepts of competitive benchmarking or strategy development. Competitive benchmarking essentially focuses on measurable metrics that reflect operational and market performance. These could be market share, published financials and stock price. The paradigm of strategic comparators and responders includes external benchmarking but goes beyond that into a holistic reinvention of the art and science of strategy formulation. It is based on the premise that operational metrics or cross-sectional snapshots of a firm or its competitors do not necessarily capture the longitudinal impact or potential of external developments and potential external-internal (dis) equilibrium. Simple benchmarks also fail to project the transformational trends that could potentially rewrite the comparative attractiveness of economies and competitive positioning of firms. Predicting transformational phenomena requires superior analysis and judgment on the part of strategy formulators and chief scientific officers. For example, when the concept of Brazil-Russia-India-China-South Africa (BRICS) as the rapid growth economies of the future was propounded a few years ago there were not many takers; however, it became a reality sooner than forecast. Firms that embraced the BRICS concept early on benefitted from the rapid and transformational economic growth of such countries.

Strategic comparators emerge as both metrics and scenarios. Strategic responders reset the firm's strategy in response to strategic comparators. The theory uses metrics as a means to predict the future based on statistical sciences and experiential judgments, given the complexity. Essentially, comparators occur at four levels over the two dimensions of economy and industry: macro-economic, micro-economic, macro-industrial and micro-industrial. For example, current macro-economic trends and social aspirations indicate major transformation for India, with the country likely to become the third largest economy by 2035, with greater rural inclusivity and all-round development. At a micro-economic level, changing demographics, which would lead to around sixty percent of the population being of thirty years of age or below, portend a major transformation in consumption patterns. From a macro-industrial perspective, new industrial sectors catering to children and youth could be the new drivers of industrial growth. At a micro-industrial level, firm- and industry-specific competencies honed in industries such as automobiles, pharmaceuticals, IT, engineering, communication, defence and electronics could become factors of national comparative advantage. Any strategic planning process must, therefore, address the economic-industrial scenario.

Strategic planning in the 1960s and 1970s advocated the analysis of the economic and technological environment as a primary component of long-range planning. Firms felt it was important to have economic analysts, including econometricians, in long-range planning departments. However, the slow rates of change in the external environment at the time caused such analytics to seem like a redundant, non-value adding exercise. Not surprisingly, strategists and CEOs began to focus more on firm-specific internal factors than on external factors, a trend fortified over the 1980s to 2000s. CK Prahalad's concept of core competencies of the firm reinforced the trend. Although Michael Porter focused on micro-industrial environment as an influence over competitive strategy, his prescription also focused on firm-level competencies. With the tumultuous changes in global economic environment, the emergence of rapidly developing economies such as China and India and exponential growth in new technologies, an understanding and forecasting of external economic and technological drivers, together with a more nimble and perceptive strategic response mechanism, assumes great importance for strategists.

Connecting the dots, faster and better

In the emerging world, uncertainty is the only certainty, and volatility is the only constant! The emerging environment does not lend itself to classic statistical and technical analyses of the past to arrive at the future. Globally, the scale and flow of business has enhanced to such an extent that for the first time in the 2000s, the fallibility of large individual firms put to risk entire economies. Strategy formulators are now expected to marshal intuition, experience and analytics in equal measure to develop judgments on the future. CXOs who seek the comfort of pure analytics, therefore, are unlikely to take their firms far; neither would CXOs who are solely intuitive or biased by their own experiences. Emerging economies could throw up new points of inflection unexpectedly. As an example, even in the matter of air transportation where sectors are subject to rigid governmental controls, and hence apparently predictable, the trio of Emirates, Etihad and Qatar airlines have grown so much over the past five years that they can today, in the aggregate, claim more air passenger kilometres than the largest established carriers such as Lufthansa or British Airways. If the CEOs of the established airlines tried to forecast future scenarios through yearly measurement of air kilometres they would be off the mark as well as late to respond.

Strategy formulators in the new era need to not only understand the dots that could lead them to the future but also learn to connect them faster and better. Not many overseas firms perhaps predicted that China would make massive investments in super-fast bullet trains and therefore, let the initiative slip away, allowing for indigenous development of such trains by China (good for China, of course). Not many advanced nations and their national firms predicted that India would double its growth rate to more than eight percent and more per annum and consequently missed the opportunity to participate in the growth and even accelerate it. Japan, and Japanese firms, for example, were so close to, yet so far from, India; they could not foresee that India could be one of the largest markets and production centres in the world for automobiles, electronic and consumer goods. Even today, despite this experience, many countries and national firms are still unwilling to visualise India being at the cusp of a new qualitative revolution, taking growth to a new trajectory. Similarly, Indian government and firms as well as financial institutions do not seem to realise that India can acquire overseas assets much more expansively and decisively than it has done so far.

The aspirations and behaviours of nations, societies, governments, firms, industries and economies as well as of administrators, leaders, professionals, employees and people in general present innumerable indicators of a transformational future; diverse futures could be relevant for different firms. CXOs must have the perspicacity and capability to see the futures beyond the obvious through multiple lenses. Before mild ripples of change turn into huge waves of transformation, firms would have only a small window of time to retool their strategies and redirect their execution. Unidirectional companies obviously face greater challenges on this front, the saving grace being that growth economies offer baseline growth in all sectors while offering hyper growth in select sectors. Conglomerates have greater flexibility to capture opportunities across the economy. However, whether specialised or diversified, companies need to reintroduce economic, demographic, technological and social forecasting to meet future challenges and opportunities and develop appropriate mechanisms to respond to them. This external orientation requires a major transformation in how budgets and strategic plans are formulated in firms.

Strategic simulations and strategic budgets

Firms would need to reconfigure the strategic planning and budgeting processes by a two-way equilibration. Strategic plans should be unburdened of needless quantitative load and certain foundational strategic elements should be introduced in the budgeting processes. To enable this, strategic plans while being retained on a five-year rolling basis must be developed in terms of multiple scenarios rather than with singular quantitative precision. Simultaneously, the annual budgeting cycle would need to be extended into a rolling two-year span to provide the potential to cover strategic programmes from investment to commercialisation cycle. This twin change would enable companies to be prepared for dynamic changes in the environment. A two-year strategic budgeting cycle, though different from current corporate practice of a yearly span, would be the required transformation for operating executives to view their programmes with the right strategic perspective. A five-year scenario-driven strategic plan might also be unusual for absence of quantitative rigor, but would enable strategic readability and flexibility.

The strategic budgeting process would provide ample potential to understand fledgling strategic directions of incumbent firms in an industry. Company annual reports, especially in India, provide a wealth of information on physical and financial parameters and investment indices, apart from standard information on balance sheet, income statement, cash flow statement and asset schedule. Some of these include information on underlying strategic parameters such as licensed and installed capacities, production, sales, imports, exports, consumption of materials, inventories, energy consumption, technology imports, R&D investments, indigenisation efforts, senior managerial remuneration, etc. Most information is also made available on segmental or product basis. The information pool enables strategists to quantify and judge trends relating to several strategic parameters such as product specialisation, export orientation, import dependence, asset intensity, research commitment, energy efficiency, import substitution, financial prudence, operational excellence and so on. By integrating such quantitative strategic parameters in bi-annual planning processes, strategic budgets equip the larger organisation to deliver operations in line with the corporation's strategic intent (see also Chapter 8 on Theory of Market Signalling).

The strategic simulations would, on the other hand, develop multiple scenarios of likely external environment, competitor moves and potential strategic fit between the firm and any of the scenarios. As discussed earlier, economic and industrial environments can be simulated in a 2×2 macro and micro matrix. Each environmental facet can be, in turn, assessed on a 3×3 matrix of the interplay of optimistic, likely and pessimistic economic opportunity scenarios on the one hand and dominating, co-existing and declining competitor dynamics on the other; a firm would have thirty-six scenarios to play around with. Assuming again that the firm chooses an aggressive, middle-of-the-road or conservative competitive strategy there would be 108 scenarios that could develop for the firm. The ability of the firm to deep-dive into each of the scenarios of opportunity, competition and competitive strategy in terms of various causative triggers could lead to even more intense scenario build-up. Economic opportunity even in one scenario, say optimistic, could be characterised by different levels of national savings, inflation and FDI or by different rates of growth in agricultural, industrial and service sectors, for example. Competitor actions could be characterised by different levels of cash generation, cash deployment and external financing or different levels of emphasis in core domains of research, manufacturing and marketing. A firm could, in each of its competitive strategies, seek out a cost position, differentiated position or niche position. The possibilities are endless; thus, the new-age firm would need a new way of organising the strategic planning function in a more intellectually reinforced way. Figure 15.1 summarises the discussion so far.

Strategy bot

The immediate organisational view should be to expand and restructure strategic planning departments into three clear specialisations to meet

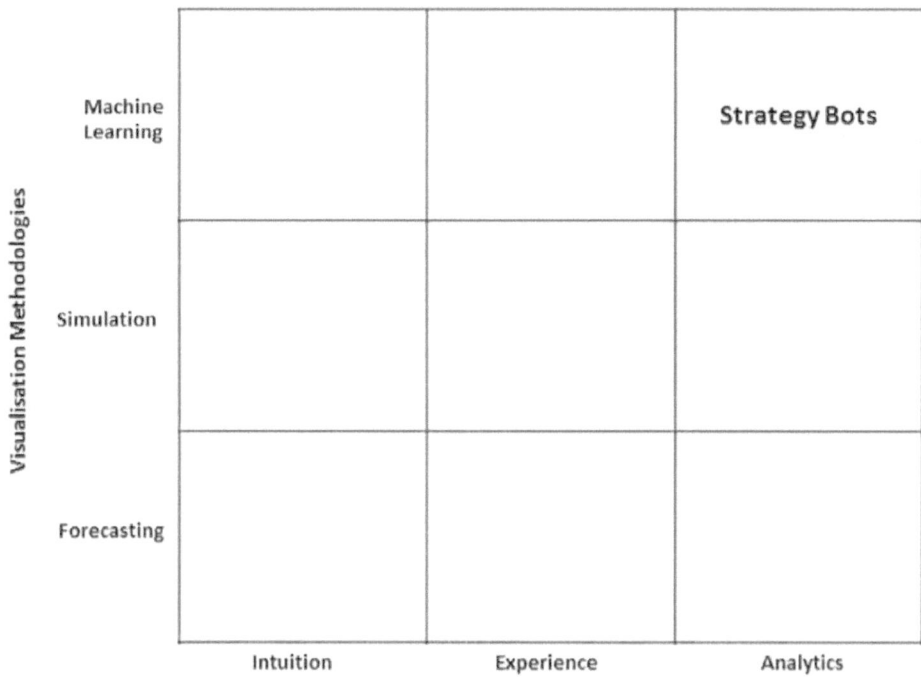

Figure 15.1
Drivers of Strategic Planning

the new-age challenges of internally competent and externally sensitive strategic planning. The first specialisation stream would be driven by economists and technologists best equipped to forecast economic and technological scenarios. The second specialisation stream would focus on competitive intelligence to identify strategies and execution plans of competitors. The third specialisation would be internally driven, analysing the firm's strengths and weaknesses and developing the firm's strategic options to achieve a fit with multiple economic and technological scenarios. The holistic strategic planning process identifies drivers of competitive strategy, in a contextually meaningful combination of various theories of strategy. Figure 15.2 presents the strategic planning process relevant for the new digital age.

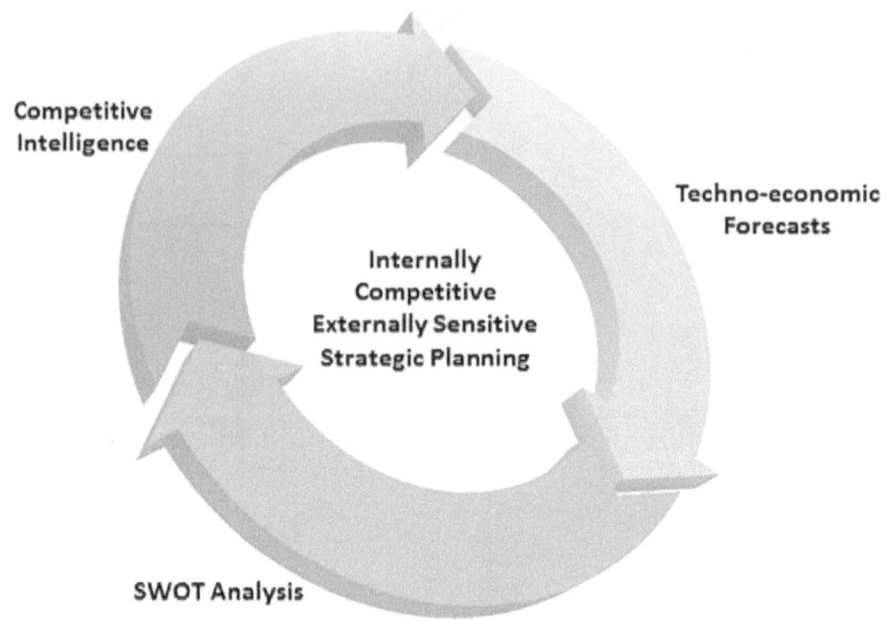

Figure 15.2
Strategy Formulation Process

The longer term organisational view should be to integrate the huge developments taking place in data analytics, artificial intelligence and machine learning to create 'strategy bots' that can pore over and synthesise the billions of bytes of data, to keep creating and recreating strategic simulations. Strategy bots would help strategists free themselves from overwhelming data loads and focus on critical scenarios and milestones. The chief strategy officer would need to be both an erudite synthesiser of the enormous amount of information thus generated and an outstanding collaborator of multiple specialists to arrive at the most plausible set of strategic comparators and the most feasible set of competitive strategies. The new age chief strategy officer must be a professional *par excellence* who can pioneer and institutionalise the new paradigm of strategic comparators and responders in the firm.

Epilogue

The Strategically Balanced Corporation

A New Approach to Competitive Advantage: The Strategically Balanced Corporation

- An optimal strategy is one that not only is open to environmental opportunities but also hedges against environmental uncertainties.
- Strategic balance must not be misconstrued as striking a middle ground; rather, it should be seen as a quest for optimality of a firm.
- Balance in value, portfolio, manufacturing, marketing and talent are important enablers of strategic balance.
- A strategically balanced corporation is able to move through the economic and business cycles successfully while exploiting opportunities with agility.

Corporations are established and developed based on a combination of vision, strategy and execution. Of these three, strategy undoubtedly sets the pathway to accomplish a vision through execution. Strategy differentiates one firm from another, not necessarily in terms of performance but more in terms of how it seeks to achieve its vision. Firms are commonly viewed as specialised, diversified, integrated, local, global and so on. Strategy, at its core, has not altered much over the years but the environmental information and internal awareness that sets the tone for it has become more complex and more volatile. The number of players in an industry has also increased significantly. Corporations are finding it increasingly difficult to develop unique strategies. Strategy, in this context, is not about which industry or business to operate in but how to achieve competitive advantage in a chosen business or industry.

For good measure, we do have quite a few strategic templates from management gurus as listed in the Bibliography. This book extensively focuses on a review of and a retake on Porter's competitive strategy as the prescription for firms to achieve competitive advantage. Equally relevant for strategy is the theory of core competence by C K Prahalad. There are also several theories for firms and organisations to become effective and competitive, for example, the model of balanced scorecard by Robert Kaplan and David Norton, the theory of constraints by Eliyahu Goldratt, the theory of reengineering by Michael Hammer and the theory of innovation by Vijay Govindarajan. However, these theories, especially the ones developed in the 1980s and 1990s, do not take into account the perfect spread of information and options that is now available for strategists and firms. Every leader, for example, is aware of the generic strategies of cost leadership and differentiation or niche and even sub-strategies to achieve them. What firms must now focus on is developing an elegant balance among multiple strategic options. This chapter proposes the paradigm of strategically balanced corporation towards that end.

Strategic balance

An optimal strategy is one that is not only open to environmental opportunities but also hedges against environmental uncertainties. Strategic approaches vary widely from planning and execution based on available resources at one end to generating resources that are required to plan and execute the strategy. A proactive strategy is a parallel process: moving forward, executing with available resources while generating resources to execute even more. This requires that the strategy must always balance rewards and risks on the one hand and aspiration and attainability on the other. Obtaining this balance is a delicate and complex process, with strategists required to be both conservative and aggressive as opportunities present themselves. The concept of strategic balance is relevant for mono-product as well as multi-product and multi-business firms. It is also not necessarily limited to products or services but covers all the essential parts of a firm's value chain such as the products and services delivered, the manufacturing or delivery process used, the customer-outreach methods employed, the after-sales service provided, the human resources deployed and so on.

Research has focused on firms adopting certain extreme strategies. For example, the existence of a correlation between market share and profitability is well researched. Unique sustainability characteristics that specialised and conglomerated businesses might possess have also been investigated. However, research on what constitutes a strategic balance and whether it leads to superior performance is practically negligible. In the context of the extensive review in this book, this chapter creates a fundamental platform to understand and analyse strategic balance. We may define strategic balance as firm-specific and existing by design among various key components of a firm's value chain and between strategic options that exist with respect to each component of the value chain. Strategic balance must not be misconstrued as striking a middle ground; rather it should be seen as a quest for optimality of a firm. The concept of strategic balance is amplified below.

Value balance

Some believe that it is not important for a firm to operate across all segments of the value chain. This school of thought argues that a firm could just develop a core competence and stick to it. An analogy could be that a firm could be a design house but could manufacture and market products with external alliances as successfully as a fully integrated firm. Such outsourcing hypotheses could be true to an extent but are not sustainable. Corporate history has enough chapters of firms that mimicked a full value-chain operation on only certain basic internal strengths and with a large extent of external support but withered away when alliance partners denied support or failed to respond to growth opportunities because of lack of internal capabilities. As a matter of fundamental principle, a firm that does not ensure value-chain balance with appropriate attention to key components such as R&D, manufacturing, supply chain, marketing, human resources and information technology would be suboptimal and less sustainable in a competitive world. This is by no means an all-inclusive listing of value-chain components. If external alliances are a must because of resource constraints, they should be structured as long-term collaborative strategic alliances.

Portfolio balance

Every firm exists and grows based on products and services in a particular business, be it hospitals or healthcare business and automobiles or transportation business. The notion that portfolio concepts are valid for only diversified businesses is archaic. Even a business of coffee chains can apply and benefit from portfolio balance concepts. Once a business is defined, whether narrowly or broadly, a portfolio of products or services can be developed creatively. A portfolio approach is based on the strategic truism that even a seemingly focused service or product offers more than just one product or service functionality to the customer. A restaurant may serve only food but it can provide several choices in terms of culinary streams to its customers. Even Starbucks, known for its pioneering coffee line of business, has multiple beverages, hot and cold, besides several eats and food accessories as its portfolio. The strategic challenge lies in developing the right balance between specialisation and diversification. Any business can be creatively developed to provide the opportunity for strategic portfolio balance: a company manufacturing only heavy trucks can offer a wide portfolio from bare chassis to fully built custom-application vehicles on the one hand and civilian to defence vehicles on the other. Strategic portfolio balance ensures an optimal exploitation of environmental opportunity and appropriate hedging against volatility.

Manufacturing balance

Manufacturing represents a part of the value chain that converts a proven design into a saleable product or service. Manufacturing can vary from complete integration to complete outsourcing. The former is highly resource intensive with high fixed overheads that could be rather catastrophic in the event of a precipitous demand downturn. The latter is certainly resource-lean with low overheads but could be highly vulnerable in the event of a sharp and sudden demand uptick. Each industry offers a paradigm of optimal manufacturing balance. A highly evolved industry where each component or material has also evolved into its own industrial structure provides several solutions for manufacturing optimality. On the other hand, a newly developing industry has fewer degrees of freedom to offer. The former implies an established quality and cost base that could afford higher outsourcing. The latter could have doubtful engineering and quality fundamentals that could demand greater control over manufacture through integration. An automobile manufacturer outsourcing different components based on availability of internal and external capabilities is an example of the former. On the other hand, a coffee chain seeking control over coffee plantations, roasting technologies and coffee making is an example of the latter. Strategic manufacturing balance ensures optimal quality, cost and delivery capabilities for a firm.

Marketing balance

The best of design and manufacturing optimality could come to a naught with strategic marketing imbalance. Marketing balance is not about regional marketing effort allocations or domestic-export balance. It is about striking the right balance between the product and the sales channel, between different marketing channels and between sales and service. Some technical marvels, the Tata Nano car to cite an example, failed to fulfil the potential of design and manufacturing brilliance due to marketing sub-optimality. Had Tata Nano been marketed through an exclusive car-dealer network, with appropriate emphasis between different marketing approaches and a special after-sales package, Nano could have captured the imagination of the target market segments. At the same time, the best of marketing cannot make up for strategic imbalances in either design or manufacturing. Godrej Interio comes across as a prime example of a lack of strategic portfolio balance (preponderant dependence on all-steel design and manufacture, as is Godrej wont); this eventually resulted in a low-business outcome, despite some great strategic marketing balance that Godrej has in terms of brand equity, distribution channels, etc. These examples also illustrate how a strategic balance among the various components of a value chain is also extremely important for a firm to achieve sustainable success.

Quality balance

Quality is a dimension on which one does not aim for balance; ideally, one must aim for perfection in quality. That said, the concept of 'fit for purpose' brings a sense of balance to quality as well. The concept of 'fit for purpose' is based on each product having a defined 'design purpose' and 'design life.' Design purpose is the specification of the use of the product; for example, stationery can be for rough use, letterhead use, brochure use, textbook use and so on. The GSM thickness of the paper is defined accordingly. Design life is the specification of how long the product should last for the design purpose. For example, in the same order, the stationery could be expected to last for single use to many year, multiple uses. Quality will need to be related to the concepts of design purpose and design life, in the process providing certain safeguards for additional use or occasional misuse. The quality-cost leadership discussed in earlier chapters has its roots in the applicable design philosophy. Even Apple which uses high calibre materials for its products, for example, has defined a clear design life for its products which has a related bearing on quality balance, but in practice the typical life extends far beyond. Firms committed to an image of high quality would go the extra mile to provide additional quality and warranty.

Talent balance

Firms are a complex cascading network of leaders, managers and executives on the one hand and equally complex network of organisation, teams and individuals on the other. Adding further complexity is the network of businesses, functions and processes within the organisation. Across all this complexity, two components stand out: individuals and teams.

Organisations are often unable to determine whether it is the individual performance or team performance that determines the total corporate performance. Talent management thought keeps swinging between the typical Western practice of individual superstar performance and the equally typical Oriental practice of consensual team performance. This leads to somewhat strange positions taken by leadership experts wholly deprecating either 'we' or 'I' in performance management. The concept of strategic talent balance requires that individual performance be treated on par with team performance. For organisations to be successful, meritocracy based on individual performance (and individual recognition) and organisational harmony based on team performance (and team recognition) must co-exist. Without overwhelming each other, 'I' as well as 'We' are equally important for strategic talent balance.

Figure E.1 demonstrates how each firm can aspire to be a strategically balanced corporation by varying its position on each of the parameters discussed above.

Talent	Industry Median		Top Percentile
Quality	Fit for Purpose		Highest Quality
Marketing	Regional		Global
Manufacturing	Outsourced		Integrated
Portfolio	Narrow		Broad
Value Chain	Segmented		Full
Factor ↑		←— Spectrum —→	

Figure E.1
The Strategically Balanced Corporation

A balanced corporation need not take a middle path on all parameters. It could veer towards the higher end or lower end of the spectrum in a different manner in respect of each parameter, depending on the firm and industry contexts.

Strategically balanced corporation

The aspects discussed above are illustrative and not comprehensive. The value chain of a firm varies significantly and multi-functionally, depending on the industry. It is important for a firm to understand and map out its value chain in its entirety and then select the components that are critical for performance. The next step would be option mapping for each function and establishing the optimum strategic balance in each case. Long-range planning exercises that seek certain goals and develop strategies to execute towards the goals would not be effective unless they are set in the perspective of strategic balance. Strategists (whether they are chief executive officers, chief functional officers or chief strategy officers) must also be balanced professionals without any biases over what constitutes appropriate strategies; for example, some tend to seek diversification and some seek specialisation preferentially as a pre-experienced recipe for success. Such biases limit openness and effectiveness in developing true strategic balances.

A strategically balanced corporation can move through economic and business cycles successfully while exploiting opportunities with agility. The journey of a small-cap start-up entity through the phase of mid-cap company to the goal of a large-cap blue chip company is based on strategic balance adding strength and resilience to exploit opportunities and withstand uncertainties. A strategically balanced mid-cap or blue-chip firm leads to the evolution of a conglomerate. While a conglomerate provides considerable flexibility to define varied businesses under its fold (for example, salt to software and chips to ships), it is essential that each business or firm under the conglomerate umbrella is a strategically balanced corporation. The seeding, screening and weeding of individual businesses adopted by big conglomerates, from time to time, is proof enough of the need for individual firms to be strategically balanced and sustainably effective. If research were to be undertaken on the performance of strategically balanced corporations, the results would support superior performance by, and superior competitive advantage for, such balanced firms.

Bibliography

C B Rao. "Strategy and Structure of the Indian Automobile Industry: A Study of the Four-Wheeler Sector," Indian Institute of Technology Madras, 1991.

C B Rao. "From Start-up to Ramp-up: Indian Insights and Global Context." Chennai: Leadercrest Academy and Notion Press, 2016.

C B Rao. "Technology and Competitive Strategy: A Contemporary Perspective." Chennai: Leadercrest Academy and Notion Press, 2016.

Davenport, Thomas H, Jeanee G. Harris and Robert Morison, Analytics and Work: Smarter Decisions, Better Results, Harvard Business Publishing, 2010.

Hamel, Gary and C K Prahalad. "Do you really Have a Global Strategy?" Harvard Business Review 68, No 4 (1985): 139–148.

Hamel, Gary and C K Prahalad. "Strategic Intent." Harvard Business Review, 67, No.3 (1989): 63–76.

Hamel, Gary and C K Prahalad. "Competing for the Future" Harvard Business Review, 72, No.4 (1994): 122–128.

Hammer, Michael, and James Champy. Re-engineering the Corporation: A Manifesto for Business Revolution. New York: Harper Business, 1993.

Hofer, Charles W., and Dan Schendel. Strategy Formulation: Analytical Concepts. St Paul: West Publishing, 1998.

Kanter, Rosabeth Moss. The Change Masters: Innovation for Productivity in the American Corporation. New York: Simon & Schuster, 1983.

Kaplan, Robert S and David P Norton, Alignment: Using the Balanced Scorecard to Create Corporate Synergies, Harvard Business Publishing, 2006.

Magretta, John. Understanding Michael Porter: The Essential Guide to Competition and Strategy. Harvard Business Publishing, 2011.

Martin, Roger L. The Design of Business: Why Design Thinking is the Next Competitive Advantage, Harvard Business Publishing, 2009.

McGrath Rita Gunther and Alex Gourlay. The End of Competitive Advantage: How to Keep Your Strategy Moving as Fast as Your Business. Harvard Business Publishing, 2013.

Porter, Michael E. Competitive Strategy: Techniques for Analyzing Industries and Competitors. New York: The Free Press, 1980.

Porter, Michael E. Competitive Advantage: Creating and Sustaining Superior Performance. New York: The Free Press, 1985.

Porter, Michael E. The Competitive Advantage of Nations. New York: The Free Press, 1990.

Porter, Michael E. "What is Strategy?" Harvard Business Review, November-December 1996.

Porter, Michael E. On Competition, Updated and Expanded Edition, Harvard Business Publishing, 2008.

Prahalad, C K and Gary Hamel. "The Core Competence of the Corporation." Harvard Business Review, 68, No. 3 (1990): 79–91.

Vijay Govindarajan and Chris Trimble. Reverse Innovation: Create Far From Home, Win Everywhere. Harvard Business Review Press, 2012.

Vijay Govindarajan. The Three Box Solution: A Strategy for Leading Innovation, Harvard Business Review Press, 2016.

About the Author

Dr C Bhaktavatsala Rao holds a Ph.D. in Industrial Management and an M.Tech. in Industrial Engineering, both from the Indian Institute of Technology Madras, Chennai, and a B.E. in Mechanical Engineering from Sri Venkateswara University, Tirupati.

Dr C B Rao has over forty-two years of diversified experience in strategic and operational leadership of large, reputed companies, including global MNCs, in India. He has led these companies on paths of rapid growth and value creation. A business leader with deep roots in pharmaceutical and automobile industries and a strong grasp over all functional domains, he has undertaken several growth-driving and value-building integration and diversification initiatives for these companies. He is a prolific writer with over 130 publications in economic and business dailies and refereed journals to his credit. His management blog, *Strategy Musings* at cbrao2008.blogspot.com, features regular articles on different aspects of strategy and leadership.

Leadercrest Academy was established by Dr Rao, to leverage his knowledge and experience in collaboration with other experts, as a world-class institution for leadership development, competitive strategy and corporate governance that would enable business and industrial excellence. Leadercrest is committed to publishing books and reading materials to support its objectives.

Dr C B Rao recently authored two books, *From Start-up to Ramp-up: Indian Insights* and *Global Context and Technology and Competitive Strategy: Perspectives for Innovators, Differentiators and Followers,* which have received critical acclaim. Both books were published under the Leadercrest banner with Notion Press.

www.ingramcontent.com/pod-product-compliance
Lightning Source LLC
Chambersburg PA
CBHW020421220526
45464CB00002B/523